Sandra Gurvis

111 Places
in Columbus
That You Must
Not Miss

Photographs by Mitch Geiser

emons:

To my family with much love, especially Hope. S. G.

© Emons Verlag GmbH
All rights reserved
© Photographs by Mitch Geiser, except see p. 238
© Cover motif: shutterstock.com/Kevin B. Photography
Edited by Karen E. Seiger
Layout: Eva Kraskes, based on a design
by Lübbeke | Naumann | Thoben
Maps: altancicek.design, www.altancicek.de
Basic cartographical information from Openstreetmap,
© OpenStreetMap-Mitwirkende, ODbL
Printing and binding: Grafisches Centrum Cuno, Calbe
Printed in Germany 2019
ISBN 978-3-7408-0600-2
First edition

Did you enjoy this guidebook? Would you like to see more?
Join us in uncovering new places around the world on:
www.111places.com

Foreword

Columbus native James Thurber said, "Columbus is a town in which almost anything is likely to happen, and in which almost everything has."

In the 1970s, my college friends asked me, "Why are you moving to Cowtown?" Well, I had a job and family, including aunts and a grandmother who had emigrated to Columbus from Hungary and Russia, respectively, around WWI. I have lived her for over 40 years, and I have never been bored.

That's the thing about Columbus. It opens its arms to everybody. Academic, scientist, engineer, fashionista, artist, service provider, or tradesperson – this city, with all its diversity and growth, allows you to be whoever you want to be. People here are friendly and kind.

Even if you don't care about college football – you know who you are – you still know when it's OSU football season. Yes, there is traffic on home game days, and restaurants are mobbed. But like the winters that occasionally induce panic on the freeways, and the summers with seemingly nonstop road construction, these are all things that make Columbus, well, Columbus.

This is my fourth book about local and statewide attractions, and writing it renewed my deep joy in exploring places that I thought I knew and finding others I'd never even heard of before, like Hayden Falls Park. I learned even more Ohio history at the Orton Geological Museum and (surprisingly) at Columbus Architectural Salvage. And I experienced firsthand the city's infusion of enthusiasm and entrepreneurship at BrewDog Doghouse Hotel.

You'll find Thurber's "almost anything" in these 111 places. Whether it's a juicy scandal, an eclectic entertainment scene, or dozens of bars and restaurants, the city pretty much has it all.

I wrote this book for those who visit or stay for a few days or a lifetime. Cowtown no more.

S. G.

111 Places

1 __ 400 West Rich

Columbus' cultural heartbeat

Located in a former toilet factory, 400 West Rich Street is now flush
with talent, innovation, and creativity. A financial consultant, a Tup-
perware salesperson, and a branding expert share studio/co-working
space with candle makers, an architect, and a consortium of Ohio
State faculty and staff looking to incubate new ideas. The place is
also filled with artists who create everything from theater costumes
to abstract portraits to colorful textiles, along with dozens of other
established and startup entrepreneurs, technology companies, and
craft artisans. It even has a restaurant, Strongwater, which offers a rich
menu that includes vegetarian and gluten-free options, and cocktails
inspired by the neighborhood.

Yet this crazy quilt of warren-like hallways, open spaces, and
industrial chic ceilings is hardly an ivory tower. It began its present
iteration in 2011 as a rundown facility with a handful of edgy creative types. Along with resident birds, wildlife, and even a tree, the
place also had a leaky roof and was an HVAC nightmare. But in true
Mickey Rooney tradition, the owners, urban-revitalization company
Urban Smart Growth, rolled up their sleeves and brought it up to
code while maintaining the original aesthetics. They began hosting
community events, concerts, parties, and a farmers market, comple-
menting the vital and funky nature of surrounding Franklinton.

You can take a workshop and learn many different life skills: aerial
dance, printmaking, jewelry design, and even trendy acrylic pour.
400 West Rich is part of the community-wide Franklinton Fridays
and also has its own end-of-month artisan market, where tenants and
other vendors sell their wares. Welcome Wednesdays offer after-hours
peeks at artists and others at work, including demos and open studios.
Three galleries showcase their work and the community's growth, as
well as hosting fashion shows and other events. There's even a photography studio. 400 West Rich is the place for creative entrepreneurs.

Address 400 W Rich Street, Columbus, OH 43215, +1 (614) 454-1287, www.400westrich.com | **Getting there** Bus 3, 6, or 9 to W Rich Street & Lucas Street | **Hours** See website for hours and events | **Tip** Taking place on the second Friday of every month, Franklinton Fridays offers an eclectic mix of art, music, live theater, and weird science. Check website for offerings/locations (www.franklintonfridays.com).

2__94th Aero Squadron
Plane to fame

Some restaurants are known for their food, others for their ambiance. Fronted by a WWII-era fighter plane, the memorabilia-laden French farmhouse known as the 94th Aero Squadron, located right next to the runways at John Glenn International Airport, is firmly in the latter camp. Patrons have been watching departures and take-offs through oversized windows at this Columbus staple for over 40 years, through a couple of bankruptcies and too-many-to-count changes in ownership. It's also a favored spot for brunch, parties, and cradle-to-grave events, from baby showers to memorial gatherings for deceased vets.

Established in 1917 at Kelly Field, Texas, the original 94th, after which this restaurant is named, mostly consisted of volunteers who, along with risking their lives during WWI by flying aircraft that looked about as stable as a balsa wood model, designed the squadron's iconic emblem of 'tossing a ring' into Uncle Sam's top hat, also the restaurant's logo. The 94th also produced several standout fliers, most notably Columbus native and Medal of Honor recipient Eddie Rickenbacker, who served as an inspiration for aviators in WWII and subsequent conflicts. The squadron continues today as the 94th Fighter Squadron, having replaced barnstormers with stealth tactical fighters.

Its namesake eatery, however, remains entrenched in the first two (and hopefully last) world wars, a hodgepodge of ailerons, crockery, emblems, flags, and other military and aviation relics, amid a dark, wood-paneled, and beamed interior made cozy with oversized stone fireplaces. Although there have been some changes to the menu, the food is basic American cuisine.

But thanks to the efforts of the original 94th Aero Squadron and their successors, patrons can meet, eat, and converse about any subject over a hearty meal. And the view is hard to beat, no matter where you sit.

Address 5030 Sawyer Road, Columbus, OH 43219, +1 (614) 237-8887,
www.the94thaero.com | Getting there Bus 24 to N Hamilton & Sawyer Road | Hours
Mon–Sat 4–9pm, Sun 10am–8pm | Tip The airport itself offers some interesting
artwork, including *Brushstrokes in Flight* by pop artist and OSU alum Roy Lichtenstein
(4600 International Gateway, Columbus, OH 43219, www.flycolumbus.com/at-the-airport).

3__Abubakar Asiddiq Islamic Center

Worshipping in the community

When you visit the Abubakar Asiddiq Islamic Center (AAIC), you'll be asked to remove your shoes, and you may also be asked to cover your head when entering the mosque, a general practice of respect when entering into an Islamic religious institution.

And respect and tolerance is really what they are all about, according to director and Imam Horsed Noah. "Our job is to connect with the community at large, raise awareness about Islam, and make sure our congregation and others feel safe and welcome." Despite rampant Islamophobia "among those unfamiliar with our culture," the AAIC is vibrant and welcoming, and full of the observant even on what might be a slow weekday at a church or synagogue. Along with regular services, they host religious classes and offer after-school tutoring, lectures, and other outreach activities, as well as a planned sports program.

Many of Columbus' estimated 50,000 Somalis live on the West Side, where the 15,000-foot AAIC is located, an improvement over their previous house of worship, a cramped, rented storefront with open ductwork, leaking pipes, and a makeshift ceiling. The 2,000-member congregation (which also includes non-Somalis), many of whom are first-generation immigrants, came together to raise an estimated $3 million for the current two-story structure, which opened in 2014. While hardly sumptuous by Western religious standards, it gets the message across by being airy and well-lit, with comfy carpeting designating worship spaces and verses from the Quran on the crown molding and flatscreen TV in front.

It is customary for women to worship separately. The women's area here has a one-way mirror into the main worship hall "so women can breastfeed and otherwise have their privacy," explains the Imam.

Address 591 Industrial Mile Road, Columbus, OH 43228, +1 (614) 272-9994, masjidabubakar.org | Getting there Take US-40 W, then turn left onto Georgesville Road, turn right onto Industrial Mile Road, turn right onto Westport Road, destination will be on the left | Hours See website for services and events | Tip Hoyo's Kitchen, a go-to destination for well-prepared East African food, also provides a taste of home to the large Somali population on the North Side (5788 Columbus Square, Columbus, OH 43231, www.hoyoskitchen.com).

4 — Alrosa Villa

When life turns on a dime

In late November 1974, Rick Cautela opened Alrosa Villa, naming it after his parents Al and Rosa. At the time, the area was only slightly marginal, with professional offices, middle-to-lower-class homes, and a few restaurants and shops.

A lot has changed as the neighborhood has become more industrial and blue collar. But the Alrosa soldiered on, hosting first acid rock, then national and local heavy metal bands in a somewhat intimate venue (capacity: 600).

Thanks to the constant presence of Cautela, the club developed the reputation of being a solidly run venue, despite head-banging, ear-drum-busting live music, crowd-surfing, stage diving, and cash-only bar. Never mind the more than occasional bar fights and the fact that the f-bomb is used to communicate here much more than "please" or "thank you."

Events took a deadly turn on the night of December 8, 2004. Nathan Gale, a 25-year-old former marine with a history of mental problems, entered the club heavily armed. He opened fire on guitarist 'Dimebag' Darrell Abbott, 38, of the headlining band Damageplan, killing him and three others. Gale allegedly blamed Dimebag for the breakup of previous band, Pantera, and would have taken more lives, but for the heroic efforts of Columbus police officer James Niggemeyer, who fatally shot Gale as he struggled with a hostage.

Cautela thought the club was finished – some bands vowed never to play there again, and several lawsuits ensued. Nevertheless, the doors re-opened a few weeks later with a sold-out benefit concert for the families of the two local victims who had been killed.

Thus began the slow climb back. Concerts may not be as frequent, and the venue has branched out to other genres, such as reggae and country. Cautela, who is in his 70s, talks occasionally about retiring and closing the doors. And yet the Alrosa still rocks on.

Address 5055 Sinclair Road, Columbus, OH 43229, +1 (614) 636-1982, www.alrosavilla.com, arvohio@gmail.com | **Getting there** Bus 4 to 4875 Sinclair Road | **Hours** See website for event schedule | **Tip** Opened in 1999 by the late and legendary radio personality Andy 'Andyman' Davis and others, what is today known as the Tree Bar remains a cozy, funky tavern that attracts both local and national acts (919 McMillen Avenue, Columbus, OH 43212, www.treebarcolumbus.com).

5_Alum Creek Bike Trail

Wading through the waters toward freedom

The central section of the 25-mile Alum Creek Trail, which connects Easton Town Center to Bexley, features a lovely wending biking and hiking path. The route offers scenic delights, like shops and eateries. You'll cross a bridge located on the campus of Ohio Dominican University, founded in 1911 by the Dominican Sisters of Peace. On that bridge, something very important was placed there in 2017: a marker commemorating the role of this creek and other local tributaries in helping slaves escape to freedom on the Underground Railroad.

Ohio had the most extensive network of safe houses along this route to freedom, which was "a system of loosely connected safe havens where those escaping the brutal conditions of slavery were sheltered, fed, clothed, nursed, concealed, disguised, and instructed during their journey to freedom," states the marker. "Wading through the waters prohibited the bounty hunters' bloodhounds from picking up the human scent, allowing those freedom seekers to continue their journey to a safe haven under the veil of darkness. Sunbury Road, or the 'Old Sunbury Pike', was home to several Underground Railroad stations along the northern Alum Creek corridor."

There is another plaque and trail at Wolfe Park honoring African-American bike racer Marshall 'Major' Taylor who broke world records and color barriers at the turn of the 20th century. During your travels, you may also find Africa Road, which was part of the original village of East Orange that became known as Africa, Ohio in the 1850s due to a group of freed slaves who came up from North Carolina and settled there. Prior to that time, settlers in the area built barns and log cabins in the woods "that served as a hiding place for the fleeing slaves who came through the village near Alum Creek," according to the Westerville library blog.

And to think you were just going for a bike ride.

Address Ohio Dominican University, 1216 Sunbury Road, Columbus, OH 43219, www.columbus.gov/recreationandparks/trails/Alum-Creek-Trail | **Getting there** Bus 9 to Brentnell Avenue & Woodward Avenue, right on Woodward, left on Sunbury, about an 8-minute walk | **Hours** Unrestricted | **Tip** Bikers and other nature-lovers can also explore the Scioto Trail, Columbus' first greenway which travels along the riverfront and has been extended throughout downtown (see website for various locations, www.columbus.gov/recreationandparks/trails/Scioto-Trail).

6 — American Whistle
Cheep trills

How does that little ball get inside a whistle? For $5, you can find out for yourself during the 45-minute tour of the American Whistle Corporation. You'll have a total blast. And at the end of the tour, you will receive a whistle of your very own.

American Whistle, established in 1956, is the only manufacturer of metal whistles in the US. The company makes a million solid brass tooters a year and counts the NYPD and Boy Scouts of America among its clients. Along with the classic nickel-plated models, they sell brass-plated and neon whistles with matching lanyards. They also make award whistles and even a specialty whistle plated in 24 karat gold. Whistle accessories include lanyards and Safe-T-Tips, covers to protect your teeth and the whistle itself.

Whistles have been around for thousands of years. The most recent iteration was fashioned in the late 1800s by UK toolmaker Joseph Hudson, who created the 'pea whistle' after which modern whistles are modeled. Initially used in a match at the Nottingham Forest Football Club, they were quickly adopted by the London police, supplied by Hudson's Acme Whistle Company.

Whistles are used by service personnel ranging from police to lifeguards to the Red Cross. The American Defender whistle is a self-defense device for anyone who goes hiking or boating – to scare off bears or to get found. They're also useful for people who like late-night walks.

The tour offers a look at this one-of-a-kind amalgamation of high- and low-tech. Production begins with the raw material of coiled brass, which is then compressed via 30-ton presses, and then onto state-of-the-art soldering tables, which basically shape the whistle and imprint the company's logo. Next come the polishing and specialized plating processes, and finally…drum roll… the ball is inserted. To learn the secret, you have to take the tour.

Address 6540 Huntley Road, Columbus, OH 43229, +1 (614) 846-2918, www.americanwhistle.com | Getting there Bus 4 to Sinclair Road & Dublin Granville Road or Boardwalk Street & Shapter Avenue, about a 0.7-mile walk up Huntley Road | Hours Mon–Fri 9am–5pm | Tip Eat and wet your whistle at Rocket Fizz, which along with candy whistles, sells thousands of soda, candy, and novelty items, including their own brand of soft drinks in unique flavors (944 N High Street, Columbus, OH 43201, www.rocketfizz.com).

7 Anthony-Thomas Chocolates

Buckeye candy central

It's a marriage made in heaven: Columbus candy manufacturer Anthony-Thomas Chocolates and the chocolate-peanut butter 'Buckeye'. Anthony-Thomas offers factory tours, a fascinating and decadent glimpse into the making of these and other tasty treasures. If the sweet aroma doesn't make you salivate, the endless rows of milk chocolate bunnies or whatever the white-coated Willie Wonkas are concocting at the moment undoubtedly will. Once the 45-minute tour is over, you will spend some money at the adjacent store and apply the discount given to you that equals the price of admission.

Although the *Aesculus glabra*, or buckeye, is the state tree of Ohio, most references are to the actual nut (also referred to by the Native American term *hetuck*, which, loosely translated, means 'eye of a buck deer'). Thus, Ohio State University sports teams and graduates, and Ohioans themselves are referred to as 'Buckeyes'.

Candy buckeyes came about in the 1960s, thanks to a woman named Gloria Hoover, who got into the baked goods business after winning a blue ribbon at the Ohio State Fair with her grandmother's aniseed sugar cookie recipe. Hoover also developed the buckeye's precursor, the Hetuck cookie, flying all over the country to promote the cookie and marketing them "on special small trees with paper buckeye leaves and pretend cardinals," according to the Columbus Bicentennial blog.

Anthony-Thomas' perfectly smooth, creamy, peanut butter center is topped with white chocolate of the same color and surrounded by milk chocolate. In addition to tin buckets, they also come in individual packets, boxes, shot glasses, and even on decorative ceramic plates. And if you time it just right, you might get a free sample that just rolled off the factory production line.

Mix & Match
$22.95 lb.
(Excludes Truffles & Sugar Free)

Peanut Butter Cup

Caramel

Buckeye

Walnut Caramel

Caramel

Address 1777 Arlingate Lane, Columbus, OH 43228 +1 (614) 274-8405, www.anthony-thomas.com, customerservice@anthony-thomas.com | Getting there Bus 5 to Trabue Road & Arlingate Lane, walk north on Arlingate Lane toward Arlingate Plaza, turn left onto Arlingate Plaza | Hours Mon – Fri 9am – 5:30pm, Sat 9am – 5pm | Tip Diehard Ohio State fans can check out Buckeye Corner with its huge inventory of official logo fashion wear, from replica jerseys to caps, tees, polos and as well as fashion accessories, jewelry, items for the home, your car, even your pet (several locations, www.buckeyecorner.com).

8 Asterisk Supper Club
Punctuating style with sustenance

Like its namesake, Asterisk can serve a lot of purposes. It can be a bar, a tearoom, and a cool place to have lunch, dinner, or Sunday brunch. The steampunk-meets-Charles Dickens interior greets visitors with a gleaming, wooden, saloon-like bar and serves up custom cocktails, such as Liquid Luck and You're Megan Me Crazy, a nod to owner Megan Ada, for whom this restaurant is a second venture. Inspired by her restaurateur parents, she attended culinary school and paid her dues as a bartender, host, caterer, and barista, developing Asterisk's concept with the design assistance of her mother Laurie.

In back is a bookshelf-filled anteroom, with several tables, including a long communal one, glowing chandeliers, and old-fashioned, scroll-like wallpaper. All this is intended to give the effect of a slower, more subtly paced time, specifically, the Temperance Movement and Prohibition, when Westerville, the former 'Dry Capital of the World', headquartered the Anti-Saloon League of America and local speakeasies were blown up at least twice, according to historical records.

The menu is equally diverse and crowd-pleasing. 'Tea' totalers will find a world-spanning selection of Earl Grey, cardamom, chai, jasmine, and more, which pair well with the traditional British sandwiches and scones offered in the afternoon. The lunch/dinner menu offers trendy 'food before food' appetizers, like sesame tuna, marinated cauliflower, and a wide range of main courses, including burritos, ravioli, grilled scallops, and meatloaf.

A typical day sees everyone from older couples to hipsters to a 'girls' night out' gaggle of young mothers. The bow-tied, formally dressed wait staff blend seamlessly with all comers and seem to know their regulars very well.

Dining alone? Pull up a good book and start reading. Donations and even book exchanges are also welcome.

Address 14 N State Street, Westerville, OH 43081, +1 (614) 776-4633, www.asterisksupperclub.com, info@asterisksupperclub.com | **Getting there** Bus 43 via Northland Center to Westerville Park and Ride to W Main Street & N State Street | **Hours** Tue–Thu noon–10pm, Fri & Sat noon–midnight, Sun noon–4pm | **Tip** The Anti-Saloon League Museum, located in the nearby Westerville Library, offers documents, artifacts and more about the history of the Prohibition movement as well as League propaganda (126 S State Street, Westerville, OH 43081, www.westervillelibrary.org/AntiSaloon).

9 __ Auddino's Italian Bakery
Sweets spot

Since 1967, this friendly, family-owned bakery has been supplying bread, buns, rolls, pizza crusts, and more for restaurants in and around Columbus. They've also sugared their way into locals' hearts through fresh and tasty cookies, croissants, and doughnuts. Although it's pretty basic looking, the yummy smells and pleasant atmosphere welcome all comers as do the black-and-white cookies and other home-baked treats, like cream-filled longjohns and glazed or jelly-filled doughnuts.

The operation involves multiple generations and long hours. Patriarch Michele Auddino, who trained as a baker in Germany, came from Southern Italy to marry his childhood sweetheart Rosa, whose family had emigrated to Columbus. He purchased a pastry shop and, along with children, grandchildren, and in-laws, nurtured the fledgling enterprise into a multimillion-dollar flour factory with its own fleet of green-and-red Italian-themed delivery trucks.

And the Auddinos were peddling the doughnut-croissant hybrid, commonly called a 'cronut,' long before it became a thing in the mid-2010s when people stood in line at the crack of dawn in New York City to purchase only two cronuts per person at a Soho bakery. Family member Roy Auddino came up with the idea in the early 1990s, according to *The Columbus Dispatch*. Only he called them 'doughssants.' Creating the mashup was a relatively simple task. He started experimenting with them on a Tuesday, he says, and by Friday, they were ready to roll, so to speak, off the assembly line and onto the trays.

Described as a "simply stellar" combination of the "wonderful flaky texture of a croissant with the light, sugary coating of a glazed donut," according to breakfast blogger Nick Dekker, the doughssants are among the top-selling items. Auddino's use no preservatives in their products, so eat your doughssant right away to enjoy its true deliciousness.

Address 1490 Clara Street, Columbus, OH 43211, +1 (614) 294-2577 | **Getting there** Bus 12 to 1333 Fields Avenue, walk northeast, left onto Fields Avenue, right onto Grogan Avenue, right onto 11th, left onto Clara Street; by car, take I-71 to East 11th Avenue, then turn onto Clara Street | **Hours** Mon–Fri 6:30am–4pm, Sat 6:30am–3pm | **Tip** Around since the early 20th century, Resch's, another family-owned old-school bakery, now in its sixth generation, turns out cookies, cupcakes, and especially their locally renowned birthday and wedding cakes, among other toothsome delights (4061 E Livingston Avenue, Columbus, OH 43227, reschbakery.com).

10_Axis Nightclub

Gayety for all

"It's Friday night...and I'm watching Wilma Flintstone twerk against a beefy muscle dude dressed as a pterodactyl," writes an unnamed author in *IN Magazine*. Someone has attached money to a belt "dropping it over the rail, fishing it down toward West like worms on a hook."

The "sexy stone-ager" is none other than Nina West, Columbus' premier drag artist and sixth runner up on Season 11 (2019) of *RuPaul's Drag Race*, among other titles and honors. Welcome to Axis Nightclub, Columbus' largest multi-level, industrial-style dance venue that, while unabashedly LGBTQ, welcomes all sexual orientations and is the go-to spot for drag performers such as West and her Drag Mother Gloria West, as well as others with names like Freesia Balls, Gretta Goodbottom, Boyoncé, and Carmen Getit. In fact, in 2014, Columbus broke the Guinness World Record for the largest drag artist show with some 55 performers dancing to *It's Raining Men*. (The record was broken in 2016 with 73 at Pride Toronto.)

Axis was originally the site of what was known as Flytown, an entry point near the old Union Station, the neighborhood of many immigrants in the late 1880s. The melting pot of Italians, Germans, Jews, Blacks, and others lived side-by-side in ramshackle buildings. With social problems and public health challenges, it was also a place people wanted to move away from and was demolished in the 1950s and 1960s.

Axis has been instrumental in helping establish mainstream acceptance of LGBTQ people in Columbus, who face struggles similar to the original immigrants. In fact, now in its second decade, the club is also available for corporate events and parties for people seeking a venue with history, flair, and great vibes. With theme nights, popular DJs, and all-male reviews, a night at Axis is a rollicking good time, as long as you don't mind a few risqué jokes or revealing outfits.

Address 775 N High Street, Columbus, OH 43215, +1 (614) 291-4008, www.axisonhigh.com |
Getting there Bus 9 or 52 to Spring Street Terminal Bay 5, short walk to N High | Hours
Fri–Sun 10pm–2:30am | Tip An LGBTQ staple since 1987, the Tremont Lounge offers
reasonably priced drinks, a happy hour, karaoke, and other special events in a friendly
neighborhood atmosphere (708 S High Street, Columbus, OH 43206, www.facebook.com/
TremontColumbus).

11__BalletMet Dance Academy

(Not so) tiny dancers

If you've always wanted to learn to dance like a ballerina, tap like an old Hollywood movie star, or simply get fit through movement, then come to the BalletMet Dance Academy. They also have a professional ballet company that rehearses in the building. The academy has been around since 1974, and the ballet troupe officially formed four years later. The 35,000-square-foot dance center boasts seven studios, costume and scene shops, administrative offices, and a black box theater.

The academy nurtures the careers of promising young dancers through their trainee, performance ensemble, and summer intensive programs. They perform a variety of traditional, original, and contemporary pieces around Columbus and Ohio, New York City, and as far as Russia, Spain, and Egypt.

And anyone can take dance classes there too. Senior citizens are welcome, even if they have not exercised in years or rely on walkers. The In Motion class, free and designed for people ages 50 and over, "cultivate[s] strength, coordination, range of motion, flexibility, and creative skills," explains the academy's brochure, challenging the brain "by connecting thinking and moving, helping to maintain or enhance cognitive functions."

You can try the introductory, beginners, intermediate, or advanced ballet classes. Or try tap, Pilates, barre, or dance exercise. Barre is an intensive hybrid of Pilates, dance, yoga, and strength training, and is a good option for those familiar with planks, pushups, weightlifting, and other strenuous forms of exercise, combined with balance and coordination. Although the first class is free, classes are fee-based. The investment in your health is worth it, especially if you continue to attend and improve your fitness.

Address 322 Mount Vernon Avenue, Columbus, OH 43215, +1 (614) 229-4860, www.balletmet.org/academy/specialized-training | **Getting there** Bus 7 to E Spring Street & N Grant Avenue, walk east on Spring, left onto Grant, left onto Mount Vernon | **Hours** See website for schedule | **Tip** For aspiring songbirds, including those with limited warbling abilities, the Columbus Harmony Project offers performance opportunities through events and concerts, along with a chance for any volunteer to help the community through outreach projects (779 E Long Street, Columbus, OH 43203, www.harmonyproject.com).

12 The Big Basket

Big dreams die hard

You're driving along Route 16, a few miles east of Columbus, when… WHOA! Where did that ginormous picnic basket come from? At seven stories high and with two seventy-five-ton handles on the top, this woven wonder is the former Longaberger Basket World Headquarters. It is also a fanciful reminder of the big dreams the company's founder Dave Longaberger once had.

The basket-shaped building, which cost $30 million, is a marvel of engineering. Heating elements prevent the handles from freezing and protect the 30,000-square-foot, glass atrium below from falling ice. Like the baskets the company originally produced, two gold leaf Longaberger tags are affixed to the rim. But unlike the product tags, these ones are 25 × 7 feet and weigh 725 pounds. Just another day at the office.

But the story here was no picnic. Longaberger, who rose from poverty, lacked a formal education and failed several times in business before turning to the handmade baskets produced by his father. Along with creating a multi-level marketing behemoth that at one time employed nearly 8,000 workers and had sales of $1 billion, he built an entire tourist industry around his tiny hometown of Dresden, where droves of sales associates made pilgrimages to worship at the altar of all things Longaberger. But Dave's untimely death from cancer in 1999 and then 9/11 began a downward spiral. The 2008 recession drove the final nail into the crate. Although Dave's daughters Tami and Rachel struggled valiantly to diversify, the company was bought out by a conglomerate. Legal battles ensued, and the company declared bankruptcy in 2018. Longaberger baskets are more valuable than ever before.

Although the big basket is currently for sale, preservationists are keeping a close eye on potential buyers. One thing is for certain: whoever ends up purchasing the 21-acre complex will have a truly unique landmark.

Address 1500 E Main Street, Newark, OH 43055 | Getting there By car, take 161E to 37E to 16E, right on Dayton Road, then left on Main Street | Hours Unrestricted from the outside only | Tip Nearby is Dawes Arboretum, with its nearly 2,000 acres, 8 miles of hiking trails, and over 17,000 living plants set in a variety of garden and landscape milieus (7770 Jacksontown Road, Newark, OH 43056, www.dawesarb.org).

13 Billy Ireland Cartoon Library & Museum

Drawing stories, satire, and humor

The Billy Ireland Cartoon Library & Museum houses over three million pieces, including comic strips, newspaper clippings, original cartoons, graphic novels, manuscripts, and serials/comic books covering topics ranging from sports to superheroes to counterculture. So it might be best to begin your visit to the world's largest collection of cartoon memorabilia with something concrete, or in this case, wooden. That would be the desk and drawing board of Chester Gould, the creator of Dick Tracy, who used it during the 46 years that he produced the wildly popular strip.

Billy Ireland was a longtime editorial cartoonist for *The Columbus Dispatch*. His weekly commentary, The Passing Show, was a political force in its own right for several decades during the early 20th century. He also happened to hire and mentor another budding cartoonist named Milton Caniff, who created the highly syndicated landmark strips Terry and the Pirates (1934–1946) and Steve Canyon (1947–1988). After several monikers, the museum, established as two rooms in 1977 with artwork and papers from OSU alum Caniff, eventually moved to its bright and airy digs on the second floor of Sullivant Hall and was renamed for Ireland in 2009.

According to associate curator Caitlin McGurk, Ohio has produced more cartoonists than any other state. The work of natives Bill Watterson and OSU alum Jeff Smith and dozens of lesser knowns are well-represented and easily located via a searchable database as well as the largest accumulation of Japanese comics (manga) outside of that country and a colorful collection of Disney art. Two galleries feature rotating exhibits.

Cartoon art serves as a mirror of the moment, reflecting the fact that while times change, people rarely do.

Address 110 Sullivant Hall, 1813 N High Street, Columbus, OH 43210, +1 (614) 292-0538, www.cartoons.osu.edu | **Getting there** Bus 2, 18, 31, or 84 to N High Street & E 15th Avenue | **Hours** Tue–Sun 1–5pm | **Tip** Located in nearby Hopkins Hall, which houses the Department of Art, is 'the handprint' (actually several handprints) outside on the pillars, spooky reminders of an unnamed student who spent the night trapped in an elevator and was allegedly traumatized for life (128 N Oval Mall, Columbus, OH 43210).

14__Blood Bowl
Mouth to misadventure

Every city has its super-scary place, aimed to challenge ghost hunters and daredevils. Columbus' might be what is variously called the Gates of Hell, the Pit of Hell, or the Blood Bowl. But guess what? It's a drainage tunnel, people!

However, this graffiti-laden legend is worth seeing…from a distance – it is not open to the public, and for good reason. Originally built for a stream connecting Glen Echo Park to the Olentangy River, its steep-angled sides proved to be a magnet for skateboarders. The whole Blood Bowl legend came about during the 1980s, according to ohioexploration.com, because of "a skateboarder (or in some cases, someone on a bicycle), attempting to perform a trick along the slanted sides of the culvert and crashing and dying."

While easy enough to find, the actual tunnel can be hell to get to and is off limits anyway. But you can check it out from a couple of vantage points, particularly in the fall and winter when there's less foliage and underbrush. On one side, it can be glimpsed by peering down a steep ravine a few feet away from a nearby Tim Hortons. The other is behind Lucky's Supermarket, where it can be approached by crossing a creek bed – very slippery when wet – and then onto an elevated, unmarked path through the underbrush. Make sure to wear sturdy tennis or hiking shoes.

What you'll see on one end is a painted red devil's 'mouth' with matching teeth, an 'abandon all hope ye who enter here' warning if there ever was one. Those who pass through the first couple of feet of the concrete, scrawl-ridden portal may find themselves plunged into darkness and surrounded by rusted steel and more graffiti and trash or rocks washed up or discarded on that particular day. Plus, if it's raining or otherwise inclement, there's also the possibility of a sudden gush of water which could also have dire consequences. Good times!

Address Approximately behind the Tim Hortons, 2754 North High Street, Columbus, OH 43202, behind a fenced-in ravine | Getting there Bus 2 or 5 to N High Street & Olentangy Street, about a 0.1-mile walk to Tim Hortons | Hours Viewable from the outside only | Tip Portal Park, also known as Clintonville Park, is a nearly adjacent pocket of respite, with trees and picnic tables (2730 N High Street, Columbus, OH 43214, www.columbus.gov/recreationandparks/parks/Clintonville-Park).

15 __ BrewDog's Doghouse Hotel

A howling good time

Brewski aficionados will find their tribe at BrewDog Brewery's Doghouse Hotel, which also welcomes their canine friends. Thanks to its viral crowdfunding campaign, BrewDog secured over $300,000 to build the hotel. Established by owners and best friends Martin Dickie and James Watt, Scotland-based BrewDog found kindred souls among Columbus-area beer drinkers and, in 2016–2017 opened its 100,000-square-foot US headquarters and brewhouse in Canal Winchester and bars in Franklinton and the Short North.

The hotel's 32 rooms include those that are dog friendly and 8 deluxe suites, all of which overlook the company's craft brewing facility for its famous sour beer. Fermented in foeders, wooden vats normally used to age wine, sour beer is mixed with a variety of not-so-yummy-sounding bacteria and yeasts. So if you love the smell of freshly mashed malt in the morning, this is the place for you.

One is never without a beer in hand, or at least available. Drafts are offered at check-in and on tap in the industrially decorated but luxurious and spacious rooms. You can also grab a quick one from the in-room refrigerator or in the bathroom while showering with hops-infused soap and shampoo. Enjoy a communal beer at the casual bar and TV-free lounge, with its assortment of board games. Further your ale education with an in-depth tour of the brewery and a visit to the adjacent, 6,000-square-foot Beer Museum, which, although mostly geared toward promoting BrewDog products and history, also provides information about what makes a great glass of craft beer.

Checking out may require sobering up. So if you slept through the complimentary breakfast, work out in the gym with its Rogue Fitness equipment or borrow a Rover for a ride around the pond at the nearby dog park. Sound like heaven?

Address 96 Gender Road, Canal Winchester, OH 43110, +1 (614) 908-3051,
www.brewdog.com/locations/hotels/doghouse, doghousecolumbus@brewdog.com |
Getting there By car, US-33 E/Southeast Expressway to OH-674 S/Gender Road in
Canal Winchester, to OH-674 exit, drive to Gender Road | Hours Unrestricted | Tip
Adjacent to the property is the Dogtap Columbus Restaurant, which, along with full
menu and lineup of beers, provides the yeasty aroma of brewing hops at no extra charge
(96 Gender Road, Canal Winchester, OH 43110, www.brewdog.com/usa/bars/us/
brewdog-dogtap-columbus).

16 Brown Pet Cemetery

Not-so-secret deaths of pets

Among the dozens of graves at the Brown Pet Cemetery are ducks (Bertha and Marjorie Savage, 1944–1956), canine veterans (Muscles Reese, Corporal Pat Sheets, USMC, and Sargeant Fleabite Smith), a parakeet (Buddy, 1956), and an annoyed-looking feline wearing a bow (Corrina Shively, June 5, 1948–July 11, 1953 – "She was a sissy girl.") And then there's, "Our buddy, Stinky Bill, April 26, 1949–March 7, 1964," hopefully a dog and not a skunk.

People today think they have the corner on the $75.38 billion pet industry, but they're wrong. Founded in the 1920s by local veterinarian Walter A. Brown, the three-acre plot, near what is now John Glenn International Airport, became so popular that in 1934, he formed the Brown Pet Cemetery Association. Incorporated a few years later, the nonprofit status expired in 1997, which was the last year a pet was buried there. There seems to be some confusion as to who actually owns the somewhat neglected site today. According to *The Columbus Dispatch*, Brown's late son, Walter W. Brown, also a veterinarian, donated the cemetery in the early 1990s and some upkeep funds to the Capital Area Humane Society, which still manages it today with limited resources.

And the place itself is a microcosm of bygone periods, although the epitaphs are consistently more flowery and enthusiastic than those of their human counterparts (for example, "Patsy: Your faithfulness and obedience made it a pleasure to have you…"). Each decade had its 'pet' pet names too: gangster monikers Bugsy, Pinky, and Chummy, in the 1930s; GI Joe, during WWII; Rusty, Lassie, and Blondie in the 1950s and 1960s. The style of the graves changed as well, from the simple Depression-era tombstones to the more ornate ones from the 1940s on, bearing photographs of cats and dogs, to the more recent flat, carved models with chiseled, almost abstract images of beloved pets.

Address 5031 Sawyer Road, Columbus, OH 43219 | Getting there Bus 24 to N Hamilton & Sawyer Road, walk 0.2 miles west | Hours Daily 24 hours | Tip More than a shelter, Colony Cats hosts a litter of special events, including a kitten shower and other adoption happenings at pet stores and even hair salons (2740 Festival Lane, Dublin, OH 43017, www.colonycats.org).

17__The Butter Cow

Churning out sculptures since 1903

For years, Columbus was known as Cowtown, and with good reason, although it's pretty much outgrown that nickname today. In 1926, Maudine Ormsby, a champion Holstein, received more votes for OSU Homecoming Queen than there were students at the time. You can still glimpse cows peacefully chewing their cuds at the Waterman Dairy Center from bustling Lane Avenue. And the American Dairy Association Mideast continues a cherished tradition: the butter cow.

What began as a butter sculpting contest at the Ohio State Fair in 1903 has since evolved into a major attraction. Since the 1920s, a butter cow has cooled its heels in a 45-degree glass display case in the Dairy Products building. Today, people stand in long lines in the sweltering heat just to glimpse, along with a yearly themed tableau, butter Bessie. Her popularity may also have something to do with the air conditioning and ice cream, milk shakes and other dairy produce sold there.

The annual offerings in butter sculptures are wide-ranging and eclectic: Jack Nicklaus, Furby, Darth Vader, Lewis and Clark, Mr. Monopoly, a tribute to the ice-cream cone/Armed Forces/OSU Buckeyes and so on. Pulling them together can be a slippery prospect, with a team of artists spending 400–500 hours in the cooler with more than a ton of malleable, unsalted butter.

The butter is already expired and inedible, so nothing goes to waste. After the fair, it's recycled into ingredients for fuel, animal feed, makeup, and tires. Best not think about that though, or the outcome for their living brethren at the end-of-fair annual Sale of Champions. (Live cows, along with all manner of farm animals, are also on display in the various pavilions.) Rather, enjoy the displays, which have included a calf with its tongue stuck to a pole for the 2018 *A Christmas Story* movie theme, and then reward your patience with a chocolate chip cone.

Address Ohio Expo Center, 717 E 17th Avenue, Columbus, OH 43211, +1 (614) 644-3247, www.ohiostatefair.com | Getting there Bus 4 to N 4th Street & E 15th Avenue, 0.6-mile walk, turn right on 17th Street | Hours Annually late July/ early Aug, 9am–10pm | Tip Continue your bovine homage at OSU's Waterman Dairy Center, which offers group tours. Learn about the facility, herd management and milking processes and interact with the human-friendly cattle (2433 Carmack Road, Columbus, OH 43210, www.ansci.osu.edu/about-us).

18__The Buxton Inn

Purring phantoms and gourmet grub

If a gray cat jumps on your bed during your stay at the Buxton Inn, there's a good chance it's a ghost. So don't worry about allergies. Built in 1812 by Massachusetts native Orrin Granger, the Buxton was originally a post office and stagecoach stop. With hewn beams and a stone fireplace and walls, the original cellar housed the drivers, who slept on straw beds. They too are among the Buxton's many ethereal residents, although the most commonly sighted are former owners and innkeepers. The elderly, breeches-clad Granger is said to rummage throughout the pantry. Major Horton Buxton, who oversaw the inn from 1856 to 1905, is usually spotted overseeing the dining room. And Ethel (Bonnie) Bounel, 'The Lady in Blue,' who, in 1960, passed away in her private quarters, still allegedly resides in the infamous and often-requested room 9, although the other original accommodations – now rooms 7, 8, and 10 – have their supposed share of spectral squatters as well.

The oldest business in the New Englandesque town of Granville, the Buxton has also been a stop on the Underground Railroad, the site of a speakeasy in the 1920s, and a pit stop for presidents and would-be POTUSes, ranging from William Henry Harrison to Abraham Lincoln to John Kerry. It was remodeled in 2014, when Robert Schilling purchased it from longtime owners Orville and Audrey Orr, who'd had it since the early 1970s. Schilling and his daughter, manager Jennifer Valenzuela, set out to modernize the National Register of Historic Places landmark while maintaining the period ambiance. They opened up the cramped, dark lobby, restoring it to the original layout and removed the heavy drapes from the fussy dining room, transforming it into a clean, open tavern with original windows, fireplace, and woodwork.

But the all-American menu and the sign with gray tabby whose backstory is lost in the mists of time remain unchanged.

Address 313 E Broadway, Granville, OH 43023, +1 (740) 587-0001, www.buxtoninn.com, info@buxtoninn.com | Getting there By car, I-70 E/I-71 N to Union Township, take exit 126 for OH-37 toward Lancaster/Granville, follow Lancaster Road to E Broadway | Hours Unrestricted | Tip A relative newcomer built in 1924, the elegant and also updated (but apparently ghost-free) Granville Inn features chic guest rooms and the upscale Oak Room, which serves up sophisticated fare (314 E Broadway, Granville, OH 43023, granvilleinn.com).

19 Byrd Center

On top of the world in polar and climate research

How did Ohio State's small Institute of Polar Studies, established in 1960 by geologist Richard Goldthwait, evolve into the internationally recognized Byrd Polar and Climate Center, with nearly 100 inter-disciplinary, globetrotting, highly funded, award-winning faculty, researchers, and students? Could there actually be something to this climate change thing?

Rhetorical questions aside, the Byrd Center studies environmental geochemistry, glacier dynamics, polar meteorology, and much more. They offer public tours and regularly host programs and symposia for laypeople and academics. Casual visitors can geek out on lectures such as, "Greenland's Shear Margins in a Warming Climate" and "A Celebration of Women in Antarctica." School and other groups can tour the clean rooms and freezers, with their mass spectrometers and other state-of-the-art equipment designed to suss out changes in the environment by examining melted ice samples.

But the center's key impact is in the information it provides. Their website offers insights on ice core paleoclimatology (taking ice core samples from various glaciers and analyzing their relationship to Earth's past conditions); paleoceanography, the study of the history of the ocean and its interactions with the climate; remote sensing that monitors Earth using satellites and automated sensors – and even more. You can view current and past conditions in the atmosphere and oceans with the Fluid Earth Viewer, open the Antarctic REMA Explorer that visualizes data collected from Antarctica, or, closer to home, check out the current weather activity that's happening atop the center itself.

The Byrd Center regularly posts videos captured by teams trave-ling through the world's cryosphere, including a 360 video that allows you to embed yourself with a field expedition. And that's just the tip of the (rapidly melting) iceberg.

Address 1090 Carmack Road, Columbus, OH 43210, +1 (614) 292-6531,
www.byrd.osu.edu, byrd-contact@osu.edu | Getting there Bus 31 to Kenny & Kinnear
Roads, approximately a 0.5-mile walk north | Hours Mon–Fri 8am–5pm | Tip
Home to the women's hockey team, the shiver-inducing 1,000-seat OSU Ice Rink has
an open skate schedule available to the public and reasonable prices. That ice so far
remains unaffected by climate change (390 Woody Hayes Drive, Columbus, OH 43210,
www.ohiostatebuckeyes.com).

20__Cambridge Tea House

Let them eat scones

Depending on whom you ask, the Cambridge Tea House is located in Columbus, Marble Cliff, or Grandview, a Bermuda triangle of directionality. This adds to the 'of another era' sensation of this charming, free-standing, brick-and-stucco cottage, a throwback to a more leisurely era and actually more like England than central Ohio.

The amiability extends to the relaxed, cheerful interior, with light wood accents, artfully spaced tables, and discreetly displayed shopping opportunities for tea accoutrements and treats baked on-site, a pleasant contrast to the formal, overstuffed rigidity of more traditional tea rooms. You'll see families with kids here, along with the occasional service dog. The well-shaded patio offers an even more laid-back atmosphere.

But the real draw is the tea, both the beverage, of which there are approximately 25 brewed, loose-leaf varieties of herbal, green, white, black, jasmine, and oolong, and the actual tea service itself. Afternoon tea is served on a three-tiered tray, with scones, finger sandwiches, and other mini-desserts. Or you can opt for the more basic Tea and Sweets, which includes scones with clotted cream and jam, and mini-desserts. Cambridge Cream Tea with scones is another popular option, and little royals age 10 and under can opt for the Prince or Princess Tea, with heart-shaped PB&J sandwiches and drink options other than tea.

But while you may come for the tea, you may be tempted by other menu items, including a fresh berry salad, spinach and goat cheese omelet, or the tea-infused orange chicken salad sandwich. And you may indeed stay for the fresh-baked scones, which come in cream, currant, and a scone of the day, ranging from Lemon Lavender and Florence Cherry Chocolate Chip to Toasted Pecan.

This welcome British invasion is also available for occasional candlelit dinners and special events.

Address 1885 W 5th Avenue, # B, Columbus, OH 43212, +1 (614) 486-6464, www.cambridgeteahouse.com | **Getting there** Bus 5 & 22 to West 5th Avenue & Edgehill Road, approximately a 1.5-mile walk east via West 5th | **Hours** Tue–Sun 8am–3pm | **Tip** Enjoy more far-flung tea opportunities at ZenCha, which offers varieties from China, Japan, South East Asia, India, and even pairs teas with culinary entrees (982 N High Street, Columbus, OH 43201, www.zen-cha.com).

21 Camp Chase Cemetery

Where Civil War veterans rest in peace

While a cemetery for Confederate soldiers may seem curious to see in the North – and in fact, a bronze statue depicting one of their number was beheaded at Camp Chase shortly after the 2017 white supremacist riot in Charlottesville, Virginia – the estimated 2,168 soldiers buried there are long past bothering anyone. But the inscription on the boulder underneath the stone arch that supports the statue states that there are 2,220 gravestones, leaving some 52 souls unaccounted for.

In fact, for many decades after the Civil War, the cemetery, which had also been an internment camp housing 8,000 Confederate soldiers at its peak in 1863, was neglected and separated from the city by a crude stone wall, another telling political analogy. But in 1893, wounded Union veteran William H. Knauss spearheaded efforts to bring it back to life, so to speak, hiring a local farmer to fix it up, installing the memorial boulder and, in 1899, helping to found the Camp Chase Memorial Association. The organization included both Union and Confederate veterans and solicited funds to decorate the graves and erect the arch and statue monument. Five years later, Congress approved monies for its maintenance. By 1908, most graves had been identified and headstones installed, leaving the cemetery pretty much as it is today, row after row of simple markers, with the monument serving as its centerpiece.

Apparently, the Woman in Grey, an ethereal, weeping spirit clad in Civil War-era clothing, likes to wander about and leave flowers at the monument and the tombstone of one Benjamin F. Allen of the 50th Tennessee Infantry Regiment. But not all endings here are unhappy. In 2019, the statue was fully restored, although the original head was never found. Once again, the soldier stands proudly atop the arch, which, rather than stating "Confederates," instead proclaims, "Americans."

Address 2900 Sullivant Avenue, Columbus, OH 43204, +1 (937) 268-2221, www.cem.va.gov/cems/lots/campchase.asp#gi | Getting there Bus 6 to Sullivant & Southampton Avenues | Hours Daily dawn–dusk | Tip Re-enact your own war of Northern aggression, after making a reservation and taking safety instructions from a professional, at the Dueling Axes Bar, which, along with private axe-throwing lanes, allows you to bring your own beer and food (309 S 4th Street, Columbus, OH 43215, www.theduelingaxes.com).

22 Candle Lab

Pour your own aromatherapy

There is something magical about candles, even more so when you make them yourself and create your very own scents. Since 2006, Candle Lab has fanned the flames of customer creativity in each of their multiple stores in Columbus, Cincinnati, and Pittsburgh. Along with 120+ fragrances, dozens of container options are offered, although bringing your own is a no-no, even if it's super-cute. "We simply can't ensure that your candle will perform safely if poured into a jar that has not been vetted," states the Candle Lab's website. Columbus Professional Fire Fighters Local 67 is undoubtedly grateful.

Making candles is a pretty straightforward process. At least two hours before the store closes – unless you want to come back later to get your creation – you can go in, consult with a 'scent stylist' to pick out that perfect blend, which can be anything from exotic (awapuhi, peppercorn, wasabi, mahogany) to the more classic holiday and floral scents. Then mix the oils, design your label at the fragrance bar, and then pour the candle, a careful process that takes about half an hour. You can also make an accompanying room spray, body lotion, or scrub. Since the cooling-off period is another hour, and stores are located in quite walkable areas, you have some time to do a little shopping, grab a snack, or have a drink or two, especially if the weather is nice and someone else is driving.

Candles made here are formulated with natural soy wax and guaranteed to burn clean for up to 60 hours. If you'd rather not make your own, the Candle Lab also offers a full array of pre-made products with scents like absinthe, baby powder, and old books (!). Your nose will thank you, as will your pocketbook, as most offerings range from $17 to $32, with some body products and other items costing even less. Plus, if you bring back their original container, you get another $1 off.

Address Multiple locations, +1 (614) 915-0777, www.thecandlelab.com | Getting there See website for locations | Hours Mon–Sat 11am–8pm, Sun noon–5pm | Tip With Paint Nights (with or without BYOB), Pinterest parties, painting classes, and other special events, Studio 614 is the place to release your artistic talents or find out if you even have any in the first place (2487 Summit Street, Columbus, OH 43202, www.studio614.com).

23_Celebrate Local
Home-grown cornucopia

Celebrate Local is a store that does what it says. It acts as a cheerleader for 300+ artisans and independent producers from all over Ohio, showcasing their products in a dizzying display of local pride. Walk in the door, and you are immediately hit with hundreds of choices in a wide variety of categories: salsas, wine, candy, coffee, home décor, jewelry, and the list goes on.

Where to begin? Honing in on a specific type of item is usually helpful, although you may be dancing around equally curious browsers interested in the same thing – this is a store designed for serious shopping. Your options for handmade pillows, for example, include one with a 513, 614, or 713 area code, a CLE Cleveland airport designation, or one with the GPS coordinates for Columbus. The same goes for things like magnets, even though you still may be pulled in several directions when trying to decide between 'CBus' or 'Columbus' in a variety of fonts or colors, or simply a map of your home base. The food offerings are equally broad, including sauces, syrups, popcorn, jams, jellies, candies, baking mixes, sodas, and more. You can also pick up wines and beers – all made in Ohio. There's something for everyone's alcohol, sugar, and fat cravings.

Real estate expert Heidi Maybruck nurtured her original idea from the Easton Farmers Market into the bricks-and-mortar store that opened in 2011, with support from government agencies, foundations, and a local real estate investment firm. It was an instant success, and she rapidly increased the number of vendors and offerings. The personal approach is evident here as well. Vendors are treated like a big family, and everyone's success is a critical part of the store's success and basic philosophy.

Purchasing artisan and locally made products helps support small businesses of all kinds. And anything you buy here will have its own special story.

Address 3952 Townsfair Way, Columbus, OH 43219, +1 (614) 471-6446, www.celebratelocalohio.com | **Getting there** Bus 7, 9, 23, 31, 32, or 34 to Easton Way & Easter Square Place | **Hours** Mon–Thu 10am–9pm, Fri & Sat 10am–10pm, Sun noon–6pm | **Tip** Rotating exhibits and offerings from Ohio artists in ceramic, wood, fiber, glass, and metals can be found at the Ohio Craft Museum, which also sells wares at annual events (1665 W 5th Avenue, Columbus, OH 43212, www.ohiocraft.org).

24 _ Cheetah Dogs
A big cat's best friend

Although widely renowned for Colo (1956–2017), the first gorilla born under human care, and for celebrity Director Emeritus Jack Hanna, the Columbus Zoo harbors another open secret: dogs who run with the cheetahs.

What seems like a recipe for disaster is exactly the opposite. Pioneered by the San Diego Zoo and based on best practices of The Cheetah Conservation Fund in Africa, these dogs become good friends with cheetahs, helping to keep them calm and comfortable, especially during public appearances. And these special cats and dogs are cute as heck. Coby, Cash, and Cullen are yellow Labrador retrievers of varying ages. "They give the cheetahs a sense of confidence," says Suzi Rapp, Vice President of Animal Programs. "Cheetahs are by nature very shy animals, and once they bond with the dogs, they become like family," as evidenced by the back and forth movements of a cheetah named Emmet in anticipation of Cullen's afternoon visit. "They look to the dogs for cues," Rapp continues.

While cheetahs are the world's fastest animals, going from 0 to nearly 70 mph in 3 seconds, they are an endangered species, with an estimated 7,100 remaining in the wild. The good-natured retrievers are energetic and close in size to the cheetahs, and they pretty much roll with whatever comes their way. You wouldn't want to try this program with, say, chihuahuas.

Along with regular appearances – usually precluded by hordes of excited children milling around the Heart of Africa's daily 'cheetah runs' or the habitat from where they sometimes come out – Rapp and her 'cheetah dogs' travel around the country educating the public as well as school groups and other organizations. Both species seem to take it all in stride, looking for treats and chasing the lure during the run. This cheetah and dog show may be the most elaborate Labrador retriever exhibit ever.

Address 4850 W Powell Road, Powell, OH 43065, +1 (614) 645-3400, www.columbuszoo.org | Getting there Bus 7, 45, and others to Zoo, follow signage to Columbus Zoo & Aquarium | Hours Daily 9am–5pm | Tip Along with a circa 1850s Gothic Revival farmhouse, the Slate Run Historical Farm has even more animal attractions as folks dressed in period costumes go about their daily chores and care for pigs, geese, turkeys, and massive Percheron horses (1375 State Route 674 N, Canal Winchester, OH 43103, www.metroparks.net/parks-and-trails/slate-run-historical-farm).

25 — Chief Leatherlips
Tomahawking good intentions

How is it that when a bunch of (mostly) white guys get together to play in a golf tournament and it rains, they blame it on a curse from a long-dead Wyandot chief? How could Leatherlips, aka Shateyaronyah, possibly be out to get them when he was killed in 1810 by his fellow natives for trying to honor his word to the palefaces?

At least the chief got a monument out of the deal, albeit a rather inscrutable-looking one. Created in 1990 by Boston artist Ralph Helmick, the 12-foot-high limestone slab sculpture of Leatherlips' head was commissioned by the Dublin Arts Council. Visitors can walk up the steps to the top, where his brain is supposed to be. A frequent site for wedding photos, selfies, and concerts, and with the Muirfield Memorial Golf Tournament being held nearby, perhaps there is some justification for his supposed annoyance.

Nor was Leatherlips a stranger to accusations of witchcraft, although it was politics that led to his demise. A friend of the early settlers, in 1795 he signed the Treaty of Greenville, ending the Northwest Indian War. The other tribes, including the Shawnee warrior Tecumseh, were not ready to stop fighting, so a group of five Natives was dispatched to try to persuade Leatherlips to join the fight against the settlers. When he refused, they accused him of causing sickness and misfortune among the other members of the tribe. After a long, drawn-out discussion, the Natives lead the calm, implacable Leatherlips to a spot where they had already prepared a grave. In front of white witnesses, who didn't see it coming, one of their number whipped out a tomahawk, resulting in Leatherlips' gruesome, drawn-out death.

Yet he is remembered kindly by both Native Americans and Whites. So, during the 1993 and 1997 Memorial Tournaments, golfer Jack Nicklaus' wife Barbara left a glass of gin at the monument as a peace offering. It rained anyway.

Address 7377 Riverside Drive, Powell, OH 43065, +1 (614) 889-7444, www.dublinarts.org/featured-items/leatherlips | **Getting there** By car, take I-270 to exit 20 Sawmill Road south, turn left onto Bright Road, then right on Riverside Drive | **Hours** Unrestricted | **Tip** Also odd-looking, the Watch House in Dublin pays homage to the 220-foot circular mound where it seems precariously balanced. Look for references to the Modern American family in cut-out patterns in the large dome on the roof (5640 Post Road, Dublin, OH 43017, www.dublinarts.org/featured-items/watchhouse).

26__CML Main Library
Doing Andrew Carnegie proud

One thing most locals can agree on is that Columbus gives good library. The system that would become the 23-library behemoth known as the Columbus Metropolitan Library (CML) had its humble start in 1873 in a few rooms in City Hall. In 1907, the system's crown jewel, the Main Library, moved to its current downtown location, thanks to a $200,000 gift from Andrew Carnegie. In 1991, the Main Library underwent a $39-million renovation and expansion to approximately 250,000 square feet. Dignitaries, such as the late Barbara Bush, attended the dedication, praising the virtue of books, while decrying the distractions caused by television and video games – something called the World Wide Web was just beginning to appear on the horizon.

When the library reopened again in 2016, after yet another $35-million overhaul, part of a larger $130-million project, it was with considerably fewer books and great clusters of windows and open spaces. While offering expanded services to accommodate the digital age, there were also distractions in the form of views of the Columbus skyline, Topiary Garden, and, for ambulance chasers and children, helicopters landing at nearby Grant Medical Center. The library also increased its efforts toward helping underserved populations – non-English speakers, the elderly, job seekers, and immigrants – through specialized classes, meetings, and outreach programs.

While the library has won an impressive number of awards, including National Library of the Year, the inscription *Open to All* at the entrance of the original Carnegie structure pretty much tells the tale. The library as we knew it was pretty much on its way out as early as 1977 when the first public computers became available for patrons. But the books are still at the forefront here, and everyone is always welcome to attend a free lecture from a bestselling author on the second-floor, sky-lit atrium.

Address 96 S Grant Avenue, Columbus, OH 43215, +1 (614) 645-2275,
www.columbuslibrary.org | Getting there Bus 10 to E Broad & S Grant Avenue, turn
right on S Grant | Hours Mon–Thu 9am–9pm, Sat 9am–6pm, Sun 1–5pm | Tip
See firsthand how a 21st-century library can impact an underserved community at the
completely modernized and recently rebuilt Driving Park Branch (1422 E Livingston
Avenue, Columbus, OH 43205).

27 _ Columbus Architectural Salvage

Everything including the kitchen sink

A $5,500 porcelain bathtub?! This and dozens of other more affordable models are among the hundreds of thousands of items that can be found in this 10,000-square-foot space, a Valhalla of doorknobs, curtain pulls, stairs and stair parts, windows, fireplaces, furniture, lighting, metalwork, and everything else you can imagine, architecturally speaking. You will find not only the kitchen sink, but also the faucets, plumbing, and the marble countertop. Spot random oddities, such as a freestanding phone booth, a mint-green dental office spittoon, and a box full of electric meters. You won't find this stuff at any big box store.

"You never know what people might need," says proprietor Chris Sauer, who opened the current location in 2011. Prior to that, he worked in historic preservation for the City of Columbus, then as a carpenter who restored his own home to its original Victorian glory. He entered the vintage salvage game in 2006 through online and garage sales, finding materials and artifacts as buildings throughout Columbus and Ohio were being destroyed or renovated.

"With old houses, there is always the challenge of locating the right parts," he says. Items from the mid-19th and 20th centuries are categorized into sections, making it fairly simple to find what you're looking for, although it's easy to get distracted by, say, a salvaged horse stall door from the Dan Darby Farm or a back patio full of wrought iron garden furniture and outdoor statues.

And that tub? "It's the only one of its kind that we have ever seen," explains the helpful salesperson. Made of porcelain enameled cast iron, this c. 1920 holy grail is a Standard Pembroke-style, full skirt bathtub, fit for bathing and soaking like the glamorous movie star that you are.

Address 1580 Clara Street, Columbus, OH 43211, +1 (614) 299-6627, www.columbusarchitecturalsalvage.com | **Getting there** Bus 8 to E 11th Avenue & Essex Avenue, head east on E 11th Avenue to Clara Street | **Hours** Tue–Sat 9am–5pm | **Tip** With 53,000 square feet of 'they don't make 'em like they used to', Heritage Square Mall hosts over 440 vendors peddling antiques, vintage items, memorabilia, artwork, and just about everything else that someone has owned at one time or another (1865 Brice Road, Columbus, OH 43232, www.heritagesquareantiquemall.com).

28 — Columbus Idea Foundry
Foundering its stride

At 60,000 square feet, the Columbus Idea Foundry claims to be the largest makerspace in the world. But what exactly is a makerspace? Some cite it as a workshop supplying the necessary equipment to create any physical object, while others view it as more anti-technology and collaborative, resulting in new ideas or improvements. Or both, most likely. Perhaps because of this ambiguity, the foundry seems to be going through a period of growth.

Still, the 100-year-old former shoe factory with its soaring ceilings and exposed ventilation, and glassed-in, open layout makes for a noteworthy tour. Part social center, part workshop on steroids, and part contemplative refuge, this is a spot where hipsters, retirees, techies, and corporate types come together under one roof. A workshop with a variety of equipment and tools ranging from 3-D printers to table saws to lasers for intricate designs, the first floor is devoted to trades such as jewelry-making, metal and woodworking, and everything in between. Classes are offered for bladesmithing, building a Bluetooth speaker out of a cigar box, and everything in between.

With a mix of dedicated desks, private offices, and meeting/classrooms, the second floor ideally offers both solitude and a chance to collaborate, although sometimes things can get a bit noisy with animated discussions going on. Entrepreneurs and small businesses can share space with enterprises such as VSP Vision Insurance and Nationwide Children's Hospital. The mezzanine level's various nooks and eclectic layout provide a change of scenery and quietude for those who need a break from all the action.

Established in 2008, the foundry moved into its current digs in 2014. Because of extensive renovations and financial restructuring, the organization worked hard to offer services that are most relevant to the community. Innovation is paramount here, and people are finding new inner talents here daily.

Address 421 W State Street, Columbus, OH 43215, +1 (614) 653-8068, www.ideafoundry.com | Getting there Bus 3, 6, or 9 bus to W Rich Street & Lucas Street | Hours Mon–Fri 8am–7pm; tours Sat 1pm & Mon 6pm | Tip Within hawking distance is the Land Grant Brewing Company, which along with some two dozen craft beers on tap and even more for carry out, boasts a beer garden whose nonstop action includes movies, concerts, even 'backyard' BBQs (424 W Town Street, Columbus, OH 43215, www.landgrantbrewing.com).

29__Columbus Park of Roses

A rose among horns

With over 400 varieties among 12,000 roses covering 13 acres, the Columbus Park of Roses sits squarely amidst the congested suburb of Clintonville. And the destination is definitely worth the journey, whether you're figuratively gathering rosebuds while meandering through the stunning gardens, attending a summer concert or other special event at the gazebo, unwinding after a heated softball game, or getting slobbered on by an overly friendly dog while at the adjacent, much larger Whetstone Park.

Originally a farm dating back to the early 1800s, the land was purchased by the City of Columbus in 1944, with Whetstone Park opening some six years later. In the early 1950s, the Columbus Rose Club and the Central Ohio Rose Society teamed up with the mayor to designate a portion as a municipal rose park. They formed the Columbus Rose Commission, whose duties were to create the plans for the rose garden and then actually build said rose garden, which was no small task.

The Park of Roses was a blooming success, popular among the public, a huge draw for weddings and gardening groups. The original Italianate Formal Rose Garden includes 'modern' (i.e. more frequently blossoming) hybrid teas, floribundas, grandifloras, and shrub roses; a large fountain; and a viewing tower. Consisting of 'old' (before 1867) annuals, such as centifolias, gallicas, damasks, and rugosas, the Heritage Garden helped rekindle their popularity and availability. Opened in the early 2000s, the original Earth-Kind Garden tested the winter hardiness of roses here (a not-surprising fail) and was recently renamed the Backyard Garden, where it now hosts perennials, herbs, and shrubs.

Best viewing periods are mid-June and September, when a second large bloom of roses generally brings back the beautiful colors of the garden against the backdrop of the turning leaves of fall.

Address 3901 N High Street, Columbus, OH 43214, +1 (614) 645-3391, www.parkofroses.org | Getting there Bus 34 to 5220 N High Street (Stop ID 1224), or bus 2 to North High Street & Glenmont Avenue | Hours Daily 7am–dusk | Tip With a large community center as well as tennis courts and baseball diamonds, the adjacent Whetstone Park offers fishing, bike/hike trails, playgrounds, and natural areas, including native Ohio prairie lands (3923 N High Street, Columbus, OH 43214, www.columbus.gov/recreationandparks).

30 Corn Stars

Unusual tribute to farming

Before there was *Field of Corn (with Osage Oranges)*, 109 human-sized ears of corn constructed in 1994, there was its creator, artist and OSU professor Malcolm Cochran. And before that was corn star Sam Frantz, who along with his wife Eulalia, donated his farm to the city of Dublin for use as a park. And even before that, the Native Americans used the wood of the Osage orange trees, also located on the site, to make bows and tomahawks.

Corn might have fallen off the radar if not for Frantz, at least partly. From 1935-63, he worked with OSU to develop toothsome hybrid strains, such as Iowa 939, that not only out-yielded pollinated varieties by as much as 25 percent, but also produced hardier and more uniform ears. Along with winning numerous awards and serving on farm advisory boards, Franz was also a bit of a deviant, purchasing the state's first Caulkins grader, that automatically fumigated the crops and "eliminate[d] smut and other impurities," according to the Feb. 9, 1950 *Worthington News*.

Sculptor Cochran initially didn't find much inspiration from the site, according to WOSU's Curious Cbus radio program. Yet his vision for a concrete cornfield was bolstered after he talked with Sam's widow and obtained photographs of "a cornfield with paper bags over the ears so they could control fertilization," he told WOSU. "And I thought, 'This really nails it.'" He proceeded with his vision, using three different molds to create concrete ears of the hybrid Corn Belt Dent.

Surrounded by offices and housing developments, the incongruous outdoor installation initially was met with cynicism and complaints about the $70,000 tax dollar price tag. Throughout the years, though, "Cornhenge," its nickname, has become a sort of Taj Mahal to Silver Queen and other popular varieties. So much so that in 2012, nobody argued over a much-needed $85,000 restoration.

Address 4995 Rings Road, Dublin, OH 43017, +1 (614) 410-4400, www.dublinohiousa.gov |
Getting there Bus 72 or 73 to 5139 Parkcenter Avenue, Frantz Road & Monterey Drive,
Rings Road & Blazer Parkway, or 6025 Frantz Road, then less than 0.5-mile walk | Hours
Unrestricted | Tip The giant, concrete dancing hares at Ballantrae Community Park are
also a "sprayground" amid boulders (6350 Woerner Temple Road, Dublin, OH 43016,
www.dublinohiousa.gov/parks-open-space).

31　Cultural Arts Center
An arsenal of artistic endeavor

Formerly the site of public hangings, a jail, and an arsenal, the Columbus Cultural Arts Center (CAC) presents an ironic juxtaposition of life-meets-art. It rents for only $1 a year, serves as a creative hub for artists, hosts weddings, and according to legend, is home to an apparition of a 19th-century woman who occasionally appears in the pottery room.

But the standout in this castle-like structure, which sticks out anyway among its generic office building neighbors, is the stunning first-floor exhibit space. Light and airy, with gleaming wooden floors and subtly colored walls that complement even the humblest endeavors, it's a little black dress of a setting for both individual displays and social gatherings. Upstairs is a hive of smaller rooms, with classes and workshops in ceramics, drawing, enameling, jewelry, sculpture, and more. Experienced artists work alongside beginners in an unhurried atmosphere of mutual support. An excruciatingly slow elevator gives you plenty of time to think about what project you might want to pursue.

The site of a penitentiary from 1814 to 1850 was razed and rebuilt in 1861 to house weapons and munitions. (Perhaps the architects were thinking 'Trojan horse' with the fancy design.) Over 100 years later, Mel Dodge, then director of the Columbus Recreation and Parks Department, toured the recently vacated structure, had an 'aha!' moment, and saw a perfect home for their overbooked, highly popular Adult Art Center, originally situated in a former firehouse. Funds were raised, the building restored and then some, a 100-year lease was signed, and in 1978, the current iteration opened its doors.

The serendipity continues with the development of the surrounding Scioto Mile, the increasing popularity of the nearby Columbus Arts Festival, and the expansion of CAC programs that draw in over 20,000 people annually.

Address 139 W Main Street, Columbus, OH 43215, +1 (614) 645-7047,
www.culturalartscenteronline.org | **Getting there** Bus 3, 6, or 9 to W Main Street &
S Ludlow Street | **Hours** Mon & Tue 1–4pm & 7–10pm, Wed & Thu 9am–4pm &
7–10pm, Fri & Sat 9am–4pm | **Tip** Nearby Bicentennial Park offers 15,000 square feet
of pop-up fountains with lighting, fog, and other special effects for kiddos of all ages, as
well as (usually free) outdoor concerts, movies, and dances at its Performing Arts Pavilion
(233 S Civic Center Drive, Columbus, OH 43215, www.sciotomile.com/parks).

32 David Beers Cabin
Making a home here

Until 2012, the David Beers cabin, the oldest known dwelling in Columbus, had been owned by only two families. But then it was purchased for $252,000 by a campus rental company. Originally built in 1804, eight years before the city was founded, by pioneer and trader David Beers, it was combined with another cabin nearly a century later and moved to the university area by artist, bicycle racer, and circus-performer-turned-state-auditor Conn Baker, aka The Amazing Diavolo. Only in Columbus. Seriously.

Still, the residence, set very far back from the street, seems well-maintained. The exterior consists of rough-hewn, rustic wood and stone, giving the appearance of a spacious but authentic pioneer home, with subtle but inevitable contemporary touches like updated window framings, utility meters, and telephone poles. It's a private residence but if the garden is unlocked, you will get a glimpse of a spacious backyard, hand-made brick walkway, and elevated second floor. You'll need to park on the street or at another metered site, as towing is strictly enforced around the house.

Although captured by Indians as a child, Beers was released and came to Ohio in 1802. He lived in the cabin until his death in 1850 at the very ripe old age of 104. When Baker came along, he snazzed up the solid oak and walnut ceilings and floors and the very large stone hearth with his own paintings and posters from his circus travels, alongside ivory and brass souvenirs from India. Although equipped with modern conveniences including air conditioning, the lack of insulation makes it "very cold in the winter," former owner George Ziegler told *The Columbus Dispatch*. "And it's very dark in here."

Although this house may be a better place to visit and admire than to live in, one hopes that it will eventually find a permanent place as a historical residence open to all.

Address 40 E Norwich Avenue, Columbus, OH 43201 | Getting there Bus 2 or 31 to N High Street & W Northwood Avenue | Hours Viewable from the outside only | Tip At the other end of the architectural timeline is the annual Columbus Parade of Homes, a collaborative effort of builders which highlight the latest and greatest in dwellings in selected neighborhoods (various locations, www.biaparade.com).

33 __ Downtown Lazarus Building

Golden Age of shopping

Deep in the bowels of the former Lazarus building, off a mostly hidden, unnamed side street is what some State of Ohio employees call the 'portal to hell,' an underground entrance to what is now their workplace.

It's a far cry from its glory days of the mid-20th century. Back then, F & R Lazarus & Company, the crown jewel in the department store chain, was the highlight of many a shopping trip. Sparkling glass revolving doors, ooh-and-ah-invoking window dressings, and the chicken and pineapple pecan salad in the Chintz Room provided fond memories for generations. Although its beginnings were humble – a one-room men's clothing shop started in 1851 by tailor and Prussian immigrant Simon Lazarus – Simon's sons expanded into ready-to-wear, built the flagship store in 1909, and 20 years later, banded with several other department stores to form Federated Department Stores.

The store became a fashion mecca, offering animatronic displays of Santa's workshop, a 'secret gift shop' for kids, and even teen grooming courses in the 1940s and 1950s. Women dressed up in white gloves and hats to dine in the Chintz Room.

But with the rise of suburbs and big shopping malls, the flagship closed in 2004, although the chain itself had been taken over by Macy's the previous year. Almost immediately, local interest groups, the state, and city banded together with a team of architects and designers to engineer a nearly $60-million renovation. The exterior returned to its former glory with the Lazarus name on the façade and landmark water tower intact, all to great praise, including LEED Gold Certification, for an energy efficient and environmentally sensitive design.

It's an office building today, but many still remember its glory days as a glamorous destination.

Address 141 S High Street, Columbus, OH 43215 | Getting there Bus 2 to S High & E State Streets | Hours Mon–Fri, although hours and days may vary | Tip A popular replacement for the downtown shopping experience can be found at the indoor/outdoor Easton Town Center, which has nearly 300 retailers, along with dining, movies, and live entertainment (160 Easton Town Center, Columbus, OH 43219, www.eastontowncenter.com).

34___Dr. James Howard Snook

Hooked, lying, and sinking into disrepute

Whenever you take your pet to be spayed, the vet may use a 'snook hook,' invented by convicted murderer Dr. James Howard Snook. Snook, who graduated from the OSU Veterinary College in 1908, garnered two gold medals as a member of the 1920 US Olympic pistol team and eventually became department head at his alma mater. He married in his 40s and had a young daughter. He is buried in Green Lawn Cemetery in a semi-anonymous grave. Only recently was the location revealed as plot 243, with only his first two names on the tombstone.

Four years after his marriage, Snook met 21-year-old coed Theora Hix, who became his mistress and the focus of the 'trial of the century' after Snook went and hit her over the head with a ball-peen hammer on June 13, 1929, during an argument in his car. Then, ever the compassionate vet, he proceeded to euthanize her with a surgical knife, claiming he didn't want her to suffer. Snook stated that he was trying to defend himself both physically and from Theora's threats to harm his family. He also left a wide swath of evidence at the scene, including matching blood stains, tire tracks – and Theora's keys.

Their three-year affair, a sordid tale of sex and drugs in a hidden love nest, was splashed all over the press. Theora was no angel herself, taunting and instructing Snook in the erotic arts and feeding him aphrodisiacs. Still, he was convicted by a jury within a record 28 minutes. The presiding judge, appropriately named Henry Scarlett, sentenced Snook to the electric chair, where he was executed less than eight months after Theora's death. Who says the wheels of justice turn slowly?

Snook's bespectacled ghost is said to wander around Green Lawn Cemetery at night. He is crying, according to those who claim to have encountered him. Whether it's over losing his mistress, his family, or royalties from his invention is anyone's guess.

Address 1000 Green Lawn Avenue, Columbus, OH 43223, +1 (614) 444-1123, www.greenlawncemetery.org | Getting there Bus 3 to 771 Harrisburg Pike, less than 0.5 miles east of Brown Road | Hours Daily 7am–7pm | Tip Along with a tour of Green Lawn, Columbus Landmarks offers seasonal walks including lesser-known neighborhoods, as well as the well-trod Scioto Mile (57 Jefferson Avenue, Columbus, OH 43215, www.columbuslandmarks.org).

35___Drexel Theatre
Let's put on a show

None other than *The New York Times* has rhapsodized about the Drexel Theatre and Bexley…"a leafy old suburb [where] everyone plays a role." For many years, owner Jeff Frank and his wife Kathy served as unofficial arbiters of taste to the local independent movie scene. The couple gave the art deco Drexel Theatre a facelift when they purchased the old girl in 1981, reopening it with a black-tie gala featuring the Depression-era staple, *Top Hat*, and a personal appearance by Ginger Rogers. The Drexel, which began life as a grocery store in 1900, hadn't been renovated since 1937, when it was redesigned as a movie house with an audience capacity of 730. A Christmas Day showing of *One Mile from Heaven* that year sealed the deal.

But times change, even in idyllic settings. Although the Drexel continued to show mainstream movies, including an unprecedented 44-week run of *Fiddler on the Roof* (1971), multiplexes had come into their own. While Bexleyites continued to support the increasingly down-in-the heels grand dame, the rest of the world moved on. Along with dividing it into three separate screening venues, the Franks started showing independently produced movies, available nowhere else in Columbus at the time. They also instituted 'theme' events – Casablanca Night, Sci-Fi Marathon, among others – that drew people in from all over the city, doubling attendance.

Even the economic downturn of the early 2000s had a Hollywood ending. In 2009, the nonprofit Friends of the Drexel formed to lend a hand to the again-struggling theater. They eventually purchased it and entered into an agreement with Columbus Association for the Performing Arts (CAPA), which would manage the now nonprofit venue. The recent $2.5-million renovation not only glitzed out the marquee, concession stand, and bathrooms, but funded a 21st-century upgrade to digital projection, sound, and seating. And the Drexel is once again a hot ticket.

Address 2254 E Main Street, Columbus, OH 43209, +1 (614) 231-1050, www.drexel.net, info@drexel.net | **Getting there** Bus 2 to E Main Street & S Drexel Avenue | **Hours** See website for schedule | **Tip** Also popular is Studio 35, Columbus' oldest independent movie theater, which offers first-run shows and cult favorites like *The Rocky Horror Picture Show* (3055 Indianola Avenue, Columbus, OH 43202, studio35.com).

36 Early Television Museum

Broadcasting television history

Who knew that people have been kicking around the idea of television since 1847? And that while some 30 TV stations operated in the US during the 1920s, less than a decade later, all had closed, thanks to the Great Depression and the fact that a TV cost about the same as a car.

Steve McVoy shares all this information and much more at the Early Television Museum. Along with being a walking encyclopedia, he has compiled one of the largest accumulations of televisions, picture tubes, accessories, and parts in the world. A lifelong collector, McVoy worked in a TV repair shop as a teen and actually owned a cable company before selling it to start his nonprofit museum.

Like television itself, this 4,200-square-foot box offers an almost overwhelming trove of information. Everything is arranged by era: mechanical TVs from the 1920s and 1930s, British sets from 1936–1939, American sets from 1939–1941, postwar sets from 1945–1958, and early color sets from 1953–1957. Many actually work, offering the experience of early couch potatoes. But please don't switch them on yourself – leave it to the experts.

Among the over 150 sets are models of the first circa 1926 working TV – a really, really small screen of about an inch or so; a mirrored 1946 'Telejuke,' a sort of pay TV/jukebox combo; early flat screens encased in pleather (combination of plastic and leather) and other mid-20th-century TVs that used mirrors to better reflect images. Long-forgotten names like DuMont, Crosley, and U.S. Television can be found here, along with unique do-it-yourself models.

TV became viable in the 1930s when Vladimir Zworkin of RCA Victor came up with the light-and-picture-producing Iconoscope, resulting in an enthusiastic reception at the 1939 World's Fair. But once post-WWII parents of Baby Boomers got hold of it, the electronic babysitter found its way into almost every living room to this day.

Address 5396 Franklin Street, Hilliard, OH 43026, +1 (614) 771-0510,
www.earlytelevision.org, info@earlytelevision.org | **Getting there** Bus 71 to Main Street
& Scioto Darby Road, left on Main Street, left on Franklin Street, about an 11-minute
walk | **Hours** Sat 10am–6pm, Sun noon–5pm, or by appointment | **Tip** While in the
neighborhood, sample a different type of history at the Hilliard Historical Village, which
has a museum, log cabin, church, caboose, and more (5274 Norwich Street, Hilliard,
OH 43026, www.hilliardohiohistoricalsociety.com).

37__Flag Lady's Flag Store

For all your Old Glory needs – literally

The Flag Lady's Flag Store sells exactly what you think it sells: over 50 different kinds of American flags. From 'Heavy Wind' to historical to indoor to jumbo flags, the store offers nearly as many types of flagpoles and accessories, as well as hundreds of international, state, military, religious, civil service, sports, and custom wavers. Whether it's an $80 'Magnetic Auto Flag with Eagle Ornament,' a $3 USA flag lapel pin, or a 30 × 60-foot model with sewn stars and stripes and costing over $2,500, the store carries all things flag – except for the Confederate flag. They stopped carrying it in 2015 after the shooting dead of black church members in South Carolina resulted in a disturbing rush of orders.

All this came about because, in 1980, during the Iranian hostage crisis, owner and Flag Lady Mary Leavitt could not find an American flag to honor her son Andy, who was in the military. Like the 'Don't Tread on Me' flag, designed during the American Revolution, the family has a long history of military service that goes back several generations. "I was told to come back during 'flag season' – the Fourth of July – the only time they stocked American flags," recalls the Columbus native, who at the time was living in Libertyville, Illinois.

So she started peddling flags from the trunk of her car, moved back to Columbus, and eventually secured enough funds to open her first storefront on Indianola Avenue in 1984. Soon, her whole family became involved in the enterprise, which today is mostly run by her daughter, Lori Leavitt Watson. While there, you may find yourself engaging in a political discussion, which can be a combustible proposition these days. People often stop by "whenever something happens with the US or there's a crisis," says Leavitt. The most important thing is that you can buy a flag here no matter what season it is.

Address 4567 N High Street, Columbus, OH 43214, +1 (614) 263-1776,
www.flagladyusa.com, support@flagladyusa.com | **Getting there** Bus 2, 33, or 102
to N High Street & Sheffield Road or N High Street & E Schreyer Place, less than a
0.25-mile walk | **Hours** Mon–Fri 9am–5pm, Sat 10am–4pm | **Tip** Helen Winnemore's
store, which has been hawking jewelry, pottery, glasswork, and more since 1938, also
carries crafts that are made in America (150 E Kossuth Street, Columbus, OH 43206,
www.helenwinnemores.com).

38___Fox in the Snow

If you market it right, they will come

On paper, it seemed an unlikely success story. Lauren Culley and Jeff Excell, who met while working in the uber-trendy Blue Bottle Coffee in Brooklyn, NY, moved back to Culley's home state of Ohio to create their own vision of a coffee/bakery paradise.

In 2014, they opened the first Fox in the Snow – named after a Belle & Sebastian song they both favored – in an abandoned mason garage in the sketchy-but-just-about-to-turn-hip Italian Village. Barista Excell, a transplanted New Yorker who hailed from California, took care of the java side of the house, importing artisan Tandem Coffee from Portland, Maine to brew up espressos, cappuccinos, lattes, and more. Culley, the baker, pulled from family recipes and on-the-job experience and apprenticeships to create killer cinnamon rolls, cunning fruit galettes, a clever souffled egg sandwich, and other rustic delectables. A gray box of a building with garage doors was transformed into an airy yet welcoming space with long, spare tables and a bird's-eye view of the workings of the kitchen. There was no Wi-Fi.

The place was an instant hit. People can actually talk to each other and even to strangers sitting next to them, and nary a laptop nor cell phone is in sight. None of the baked goods are labeled, so learning their provenance also requires conversation with the employees. Since just about everything offered is carb-loaded, Weight Watchers and the keto diet are left behind. It is almost like…the 1950s?

Between having babies, Culley and Excell also birthed two more outposts, one in German Village that same year and another in New Albany in 2019. While they kept the same basic concept, the exterior of each reflects the flavor of its home neighborhood.

Starting any enterprise can be risky and takes grit, determination, and imagination. And while timing helps too, these two saw a low-tech opportunity and went for it.

Address See website for location addresses | Hours Mon–Fri 7am–5pm, Sat & Sun 8am–5pm | Tip Columbus also has trendy, twin breakfast places for the hipster and millennial crowd, Drunch (995 N 4th Street, Columbus, OH 43201, www.druncheatery.com) and Clintonville-based Blunch (2973 N High Street, Columbus, OH 43202, www.blunchcolumbus.com).

39 __ Friendship Park Gahanna

At the 'fore' front of black innovation

Friendship Park is a 23-acre retreat tucked away behind the back streets of old Gahanna, with sports activities, a shelter area, gazebo, and playground, and creek access for canoeing and fishing. But many may overlook its most important aspect: a single concrete set of stairs, the only remnant of the Big Walnut Country Club, which was one of the very first country clubs in the United States that catered to a Black clientele.

Established in the still-segregated mid-1920s, Big Walnut came about when Columbus' Black leaders purchased the land on a floodplain in the then-remote suburb. Influenced by the popularity of country clubs for Whites and buoyed by the Harlem Renaissance, they aimed for the same athletic and social offerings as Whites-only clubs but with "less exclusionary practices and more emphasis on the recreation and retreat aspect," according to an article in the Columbus *African-American News Journal.*

Over the next four decades it was a roaring success, with a clubhouse, a golf course with a driving range, and activities that included croquet, volleyball, and even Little League championships. The club also held dances and festivals, and even hosted beauty pageants in the 1950s for Black contestants.

Several factors contributed to its demise, including the 1955 death of a popular, influential club manager, and more significantly, the decision in the 1960s by the City of Gahanna to exercise its easement rights for the adjacent land, which "ultimately restricted access to [the club's] driveway, parking lot, and club grounds," states the article. By the 1970s, the City of Gahanna not only owned all of the land but razed the buildings, which had been damaged by floods.

Today, the newly finished Story Trail offers a kid-friendly walking history of the club, and there's a scrapbook of clippings from its heyday available at the Mayor's office. It's a start.

Address 150 Oklahoma Avenue, Gahanna, OH 43230, +1 (614) 342-4250, www.gahanna.gov | Getting there Bus 25 to Granville Street & Lincoln Circle | Hours Daily 6am–10pm | Tip Also of historical importance is the Isabelle Ridgway Care Center, whose namesake established the first successful Black 'old folks home' in Columbus in 1912. The home is not open to the public, but it's worth driving by and paying homage to its history (1520 Hawthorne Avenue, Columbus, OH 43203).

40_Glass Axis
Art with glass roots

Want to learn how to fashion a sculpture out of solid glass? Create a mosaic? Form glass beads or construct custom designs? Glass Axis is the place to go. Established in 1987 as a mobile unit by 10 'cling-ons' – Ohio State students and graduates who needed a location other than the college to practice their craft – the transparent nonprofit has grown into one of the world's top public glass art studios.

And it offers more than classes in hot and cold glass, torching/flame-working, and fusing/kiln forming. Along with hosting professional glass artists from around the world, who also provide hands-on instruction and demonstrations, the 12,700-square-foot enterprise, which moved to Franklinton in 2014, provides a full array of equipment that would otherwise be too expensive or inaccessible for many artists. Specifically the studio itself consists of "a comprehensive glass-making facility, encompassing molten glass, casting, fusing, neon, stained glass, cold working, and torch working," per their website. Safety equipment is required, for obvious reasons, so be prepared to suit up in the required gear.

The relatively new digs have fired up Glass Axis' visibility to include an industrial chic event space ideal for corporations and private parties, and a gift shop and gallery loaded with one-of-a-kind creations. Rotating exhibitions feature, for example, the glass art stylings of local school children, and a 'Glassquerade' event offers up a beer tasting and on-the-spot glass creations, although imbibing too much of the former might be catastrophic for the latter. The studio also has a steady presence at local festivals, Franklinton Fridays, and galleries.

So it should come as no surprise that Glass Axis is blowing up, in terms of business, employees, and volunteers, and also in its providing access to folks who might otherwise not be exposed to a beautiful, challenging, and often cost-prohibitive art form.

Address 610 W Town Street, Columbus, OH 43215, +1 (614) 291-4250, www.glassaxis.org, hello@glassaxis.org | **Getting there** Bus 3, 6, or 9 to W Rich Street & S Skidmore Street | **Hours** Tue–Thu 11am–6pm, Fri 11am–7pm, Sat 11am–4pm | **Tip** The OSU Urban Arts space showcases the talents of both the university and the community at large through exhibitions, outreach, and other events and is especially noted for its summer camp and kids' programs (50 W Town Street, Suite 130, Columbus, OH 43215, uas.osu.edu).

41 __ Governor's Residence
Political finery and not-so-finery

One would not expect the residence of the governor of the State of Ohio to be inhabited by prisoners, silverfish, and melted wiring. But various governors and their families were faced with these and other calamities, although the inmates were part of a program initiated by Governor Michael DiSalle (1959–1963). The program was for prisoners serving life sentences for murder, and some actually resided at the mansion, a decidedly uncomfortable situation, at least initially. Nonviolent offenders were still serving time there when Ted Strickland became governor in 2010, although security checks had been removed. A liquor and tobacco-smuggling scandal ensued, and the inmate program went into permanent lockdown.

Today the circa 1920 Jacobean-style residence has retained much of its grand and spacious ambiance, with beautiful wood accents, stained-glass windows, and a lovely garden. Some furnishings and artwork were created by native Ohioans throughout the decades, providing an unexpectedly homemade and lived-in feel. Originally owned by businessman Malcolm Jeffrey and his family, the mansion was eventually passed on to a distant Illinois relative in the 1950s, who offered it to the state. But by 1975, then-governor James Rhodes chose to live elsewhere, citing problems with leaks and heating.

Eight years later, when successor Dick Celeste and his family moved in, it was more like a house of horrors. The Celestes established the nonprofit Friends of the Residence, which helped renovate and modernize the structure. Along with getting it listed on the National Register of Historic Places, the Celestes initiated public Tuesday Tours. Although Governor John Kasich chose not to live there during his tenure, his replacement, Mike DeWine and his family can rest easy, knowing that the state will take care of the rotting timbers and leaky roof of their convict-free home.

Address 358 N Parkview Avenue, Columbus, OH 43209, +1 (614) 644-7644,
www.governorsresidence.ohio.gov/home.aspx, residence@governor.ohio.gov | Getting there
Bus 10 to E Broad Street & S Parkview Avenue, walk west on E Broad Street toward
S Parkview, turn right onto N Parkview, about a 0.6-mile walk | Hours Tue 11am &
1:30pm; tours by appointment only | Tip While at the mansion, get landscaping ideas at the
Ohio Heritage Garden, with plants representing the state's five physiographic regions in an
expansive green space resembling their natural habitats (358 N Parkview Avenue, Columbus,
OH 43209).

42__Hanby House
Of fugitive slaves and earworms

Intelligent and accomplished, the Hanbys of Westerville were also altruistic. So, although filled with 19th-century papers, memorabilia, stern-looking photos, and furniture, their smallish, rather humble abode both exudes a sense of history and feels like a home. They also produced the most persistent earworm ever.

Built in 1846, the house was purchased in 1853 by Bishop William Hanby and his wife Ann. A preacher, publisher, and avid Abolitionist, William quickly established his abode as a stop on the Underground Railroad. He also co-founded Otterbein University, a small, prominent liberal arts college, so his eight children could attend, including his daughters, who went on to careers of their own. But the tribe's standout was oldest son Ben, another preacher/Abolitionist who was also a composer. His first hit, "Darling Nellie Grey" (1856) was a true story about a runaway slave. Eight years later, he wrote "Santa Claus", now known as "Up on the Rooftop" (Click! Click! Click!). And so it began.

Music-loving, liberal Ben didn't fit into the strict Methodist preacher mode, so in 1865, he and his family moved to Chicago to accept what must have been a dream job working for a music company, although he passed away less than two years later at age 33. Bishop William Hanby drowned his sorrows by crusading for temperance, and he became heavily involved in the Westerville Whisky Wars of 1870s. The house eventually fell into disrepair and was relocated twice, moving to its current site in the 1930s after Westerville native and eventual curator Dacia Shoemaker made it her life's mission to restore it and preserve local history. Eventually, it was taken over by the Ohio Historical Society and managed by the Westerville Historical Society.

Today, visitors can attend Civil War-era teas and view a piano similar to the one on which Ben composed his music.

Address 160 W Main Street, Westerville, OH 43081, +1 (614) 891-6289, www.hanbyhouse.org, hanbyhouse@yahoo.com | **Getting there** Bus 43 to Westerville Park & Ride, walk west and turn left onto Collegeview Road, then left again on Main Street, about a 0.4-mile walk | **Hours** Tours by appointment only | **Tip** Take a tour of the cluster of 20 homes making up Westerville's Temperance Row Historic District, designed with wholesome home life and social reform in mind (126 S State Street, Westerville, OH 43081, www.westervillehistory.org).

43___Hayden Falls Park

Know the destination, then take the journey

What is 35 feet tall, surrounded by a boardwalk and one of the city's most congested suburbs, and really hard to find unless you know exactly what you are looking for? Hayden Falls!

It is 'gorge'ous, a mini-Niagara-like cascade of misty water rushing over rocks into a glistening bottom pool. Sheltered in the summer and early fall by a thick, verdant array of trees, its ecosystem consists of endangered species, such as rock cress, along with ubiquitous honeysuckle shrubs and garlic mustard. Equally ever-present are the two-legged species, a cross-section of teenagers posing for selfies, large family groups with reluctant toddlers in tow, and even an occasional photo fashion shoot of bikini-clad models.

Columbus' worst-kept secret is very popular, especially on nice days, even though it is a challenge to find. It's actually located at Grigg's Nature Preserve, off of a tiny parking lot. Part of the larger Griggs Reservoir Park, which includes over two miles of trails, a nature preserve, and a boat launch area, the Nature Preserve can be found on the west side of the Scioto River, just along Hayden Run Road and west of Griggs Reservoir bridge.

The payoff is worth the effort. Steps and the two-minute walk along an elevated path constructed in 2006 by the City of Columbus will take you past a leafy, burbling stream that looks especially tempting on hot days, although it is designed to protect the ecosystem and minimize erosion.

Best just to head over to the falls and enjoy the view and natural air conditioning. Then relax or do some serious people watching with a meal, a snack, or simply with friends and family at one of the nearby picnic tables. You can also opt for other spots to chill throughout the Reservoir Park, which attracts its share of sunbathers, hikers, athletes, and other representations of humanity and has a lot more parking.

Address 4326 Hayden Run Road, Dublin, OH 43017, www.columbus.gov/recreationandparks | Getting there Bus 21 or 72 to 3166 Hayden Road or Frantz Road & McGrath Drive, walk less than 0.4 miles | Hours Daily 8am–11pm | Tip Easier to find and almost as dramatic is Indian Run Falls, which offers the bonus of a looping trail to explore the surrounding park and river (700 Shawan Falls Drive, Dublin, OH 43017, www.dublinohiousa.gov/parks-open-space).

44_Hills Market Downtown
Local roots

The late Nancy and Roy Kerscher originally established The Hills Market in 1993 in Worthington, and it wasn't until nearly 20 years later that the second outpost opened downtown. Today, both locations are alive with the sound of satisfied customers. Vast, well-curated selections of locally sourced foodstuffs combined with location, location, location have been crucial to their success. Wine tastings, cooking classes, and other special events also make heading for these hills an adventure rather than a chore.

Located in the middle of the booming Discovery District, the downtown Hills, while smaller at 12,000 square feet, is crammed to the rafters with regional temptations. Office workers, students from Columbus State, and even a few folks who look like they've seen better days line up for carryout meals at display cases loaded with everything from curried chicken salad and Pad Thai, to vegetable empanadas. In-house and local breads share space with a gravity-defying, six-layer chocolate cake. The majority of offerings are Ohio born and/or bred. Fresh produce and poultry; towers of locally produced beers and wines; and dried fruit and cheeses direct from Ohio's Amish country induce the desire to sample or at least learn more about them.

Unlike Trader Joe's, Kroger's, Whole Foods, or other chains owned by giant corporations, Hills was purchased by employees when Nancy Kerscher retired in the mid-2000s. So personal service is king (and queen), as evidenced by the attention that workers give when fielding questions about 4,000 different wine labels, over 2,500 Ohio products, and tens of thousands of specialty items. Along with a floral shop and online ordering, gift baskets and catering are also offered.

While you may go into The Hills with the intent of purchasing a head of lettuce, you'll likely also come out with something completely unexpected.

Address 95 N Grant Avenue, Columbus, OH 43215, +1 (614) 702-7900,
www.thehillsmarket.com/downtown | Getting there Bus 10 to E Broad Street & S Grant
Street, walk east on E Broad, then turn left on N Grant Street, about a 4-minute walk |
Hours Mon–Fri 7am–9pm, Sat & Sun 9am–8pm | Tip Established by two brothers in
1961, Weiland's Market still offers a mom-and-pop grocery experience, although it's grown
from a small storefront to nearly 18,000 square feet (3600 Indianola Avenue, Columbus,
OH 43214, www.weilandsmarket.com).

45__Hockey Cannon
Blue Jackets fodder

Of course a hockey team named after Ohio's contribution of more residents to the Union Army than any other state during the Civil War would want a cannon. Not only would it annoy and unsettle the opposing team, but it's loud. And nobody does loud better than the National Hockey League (NHL). Although the Blue Jackets played their first season in 2007, the cannon didn't come on board until seven years later. "It had been tossed back and forth if we should get it or not," arena host Mike Todd told Foxsports.com. This wasn't brain surgery, and timing was never an issue. Plus by then, the Internet, which is how they located the cannon, was a lot more sophisticated than when the team first organized in 1997.

It's not an actual 1857 cannon, but a faithful reproduction by Civil War reenactment gunsmith Chris Olson of Illinois. When it was demonstrated, Olson first used cannon powder and then switched to more explosive gunpowder, after which, "the cannon recoiled about two feet," Todd continued. "It was the real deal – it sounded like doom itself." The NHL equivalent of the perfect little black dress.

The cannon is fired when the game begins and when the Blue Jackets score a goal. Sometimes, like when they score several goals in a row, it can get a little intense, even for the avid fans who flock for pre- and post-game pictures with it. To ensure public safety (but not hearing loss), the cannon receives regular maintenance, pyrotechnics are used instead of munitions, and a Columbus fire official is always on hand.

The crowd is also given a warning of sorts. After a goal, once the horn blows and AC/DC's "For Those About to Rock" starts blasting, covering your ears before vocalist Brian Johnson sings "Fire" is a good strategy. Sitting as far away from Section 111 where the cannon is located is another. Or you could just stay home and turn down (or up) the volume.

Address 200 W Nationwide Boulevard, Columbus, OH 43215, www.jacketscannon.com | **Getting there** Bus 3 to Nationwide & McConnell Boulevards, walk west on Nationwide, turn right on McConnell | **Hours** See website for game schedule | **Tip** More boisterousness can be found at the nearby Big Bang Dueling Piano Bar, which, along with the tickling of rival ivories, offers comedy and alcohol-fueled sing-alongs (401 N Front Street, Columbus, OH 43215, www.thebigbangbar.com).

46__Home of the Clippers
Huntington Park's minor league home run

Named the '2009 Ballpark of the Year' when it first opened, the 10,100-seat Huntington Park is home to the Columbus Clippers, the AAA baseball farm team for the Cleveland Indians. Initially established in 1886 as the Buckeye Baseball Club and having gone through many affiliations and franchises, this newest iteration seems to have won the World Series in aesthetics, design, and amenities, including, but far beyond, home runs and hot dogs.

The playing field is sunken so folks on the sidewalk can watch the game for free through openings in the outfield wall. But go ahead and spring the $7 or so for admission. There's not a bad seat to be found. For a bit more, you can take a seat at one of the two full bars, or at the rooftop and right field terraces. There are also picnic tables, a children's area, and wading fountains.

Clearly, food is an important part of baseball. You'll find inexpensive and varied food selections here, even at concession stands, which offer basic dogs and burgers, plus healthy grub, mostly $10 and under. City Barbecue and the Hall of Fame Grill are among the many popular on-site eateries with their massive craft 'n' draft brew array.

Markers honoring past and present Columbus players are scattered throughout the concourse. Other highlights include the Victory Bell, a firehouse bell rung during 1950s games, and a statue of 20th-century baseball booster Harold Cooper. A mural depicting the evolution of Columbus ballparks can be found behind City Barbecue, and the Hall of Fame boasts a large collection of old photos, playing equipment, and other memorabilia. So if the Clippers are having a slow inning or several, these spots are a good diversion.

With reclaimed urban land, use of historic brick to evoke that 'old time' ballpark feel, and with energy and water efficiency incorporated into the design, there's more 'green' here than on the field.

Address 330 Huntington Park Lane, Columbus, OH 43215, +1 (614) 462-5250, www.milb.com/columbus | Getting there Bus 3 or 8 to Neil Avenue & Broadbelt Lane, or SmartBlue bus to stadium | Hours See website for schedule | Tip Diehard fans get their chance to play in the big leagues at the annual Adult Baseball Fantasy Camp, which also includes meeting coaches and getting lots of swag and autographs (330 Huntington Park Lane, Columbus, OH 43215, www.milb.com/columbus/fans/fantasy-camp).

47__Homer Bostwick's Portrait
Bad boy judge

His sepia portrait on the wall of the Franklin County Probate Court-house looks like every other magistrate's. But Judge Homer Bostwick, who was elected in 1917 and enjoyed high prominence until his ouster in 1931, let his vices get in the way. To begin with, the 55-year-old adjudicator weighed some 380 pounds, which may have been due to stress eating because of the seemingly terminal illness of wife Estella. Or not. When a lawyer buddy introduced him to 24-year-old Opal Eversole, they commenced a romance immediately. Along with painting the town red, during their one-month relationship, Homer bought her an automobile and gave her Estella's diamond ring, which he figured Estella probably wouldn't miss anyway.

Estella recovered.

Homer knew he had some explaining to do regarding the ring's whereabouts. So when Opal showed up at the courthouse to obtain a marriage license with another man, a 'friend of Homer's' did some digging and found that Opal had had several prior weddings. So, with the allegation that she had made a false statement by failing to reveal her previous marriages, Opal was dragged into the prosecutor's office. When she refused to hand over the ring, she was thrown into jail. Only when Opal's intended laid the ring on the prosecutor's desk did the problem disappear.

Or so Homer thought. The now-defunct *Columbus Citizen Journal* got wind of the matter and complained to the court, seeking Bostwick's removal from the bench. (Bostwick was buddies with the publisher of the rival paper, *The Columbus Dispatch*, which only began serious coverage after the scandal became public.) Along with losing his judgeship, Bostwick was eventually disbarred, and the court put in place strict morality and conduct rules for probate judges. Bostwick remained married to Estelle until he passed away in 1957. She lived another 10 years. Apparently, karma has its own set of laws.

Address Franklin County Probate Court, 22nd Floor, 373 S High Street, Columbus, OH 43215, +1 (614) 525-3894, www.probate.franklincountyohio.gov, probate@franklincountyohio.gov | **Getting there** Bus 4 to S High Street & W Mound Street | **Hours** Call for hours | **Tip** Involvement with teams, sports, and activities at the tennis, racquetball, and wallyball courts at the Racquet Club of Columbus might not only help avoid the kind of weight problem Bostwick had but also other probate-related misadventures (1100 Bethel Road, Columbus, OH 43220, www.racquetclub1.com).

48_Hoover Reservoir Park

An industrial and natural paradise

Stand on the walkway atop Hoover Reservoir for a mini vacation. On one side is a steep gorge with tumbling waters and massive clusters of trees, a particularly stunning view, especially when the leaves turn in fall.

Fitness buffs race up and down the stairs leading to the dam, while slower paced walkers can use a smooth surface adjoining the steps. On the other side is a seemingly endless, calm expanse of water with boats and an occasional fisherman along the shore. Miles of paved bike and walking paths weave in and out of the surrounding 4,700-acre park, which includes children's play areas, observation decks, boat launches and sports fields for baseball and soccer along with picnic tables and grills to help make a day of it.

Built in the mid-1950s, as a result of the increased water demand in postwar Columbus, the project was named after two brothers, Charles and Clarence Hoover, who helped pioneer a water filtration and softening system nearly 50 years earlier that's still in use today. So while the water is fit to drink, swimming is prohibited.

The area welcomes an abundance of birds, including ducks, herons, shorebirds, warblers, and robust Canadian geese that may hiss at humans who come too close during nesting season. Birders will also find Hoover Park a mini paradise, with a half-dozen spots to perch and catch glimpses of the bald eagles, peregrine falcons, snowy owls, and scores of other species.

Perhaps the park's most unusual feature is its 27-hole disc golf course, that surprisingly popular mashup of Frisbee and traditional golf. Along with being among the first and largest in the country, the course is the site of several tournaments and maintained by the city and local disc golf club, the Columbus Flyers. When not cordoned off during official competitions or practice, the course is open to families and casual players.

Address 7701 Sunbury Road, Westerville, OH 43081, +1 (614) 645-3300, www.columbus.gov/recreationandparks | **Getting there** By car, take I-270 to OH 3S, turn left on Dempsey Road, and left on Sunbury Road | **Hours** Daily 7am–11pm | **Tip** It's smooth sailing for all ages at Hoover Sailing Club, which provides classes, facilities, and special racing events at the lake adjacent to the park (4250 Smothers Road, Westerville, OH 43082, www.hooversailingclub.com).

49__Huli Huli Lounge
Where it's tropical year-round

Although two beloved tiki bars, the Grass Skirt Tiki Room and the Kahiki, are no longer with us, the Huli Huli Tiki Lounge is still serving up Zombies, Blue Hawaiis, and other classic tiki cocktails. You get to keep your souvenir glass too!

The Huli Huli also offers also offer small plates of Hawaiian cuisine, including authentic Spam sliders and traditional puaa puaa bao pork, in a tastefully curated space designed for the 21st century. A subtly lit bi-level layout with bamboo accents, well-placed masks, colorful lamps, and other South Pacific art add an innovative layer of sophistication to traditional tiki kitsch.

The often-cheesy agglomeration of Hawaiian and Polynesian pop culture known as tiki is mostly an American fantasy that began in 1934 with Don's Beachcomber Cafe in Hollywood. Tiki grew in popularity after GIs returned from the (actual) South Pacific in WWII. It came to Columbus in 1961 with the opening of the beloved Kahiki. A King Kong-sized Polynesian war canoe designed to ward off evil spirits, it was an almost instant landmark drawing people from all over. And among the approximately 30 libations were a Mystery Drink, a bowl-sized drink meant to be shared by four, consisting of 80-proof rum, amaretto, vodka, tequila, and triple sec, with a juice chaser. A gong sounded as it was served by a scantily clad Mystery Girl. The Kahiki was torn down in 2000, much to the dismay of preservationists and its legions of fans.

Huli Huli was created with original tiki in mind, and to that end General Manager Nate Howe researched ingredients and recipes of classic cocktails of the 1940s. Howe also creates and collects custom tiki items. "We're trying to collect authentic pieces from artists and some historic pieces as well," he told *Columbus Underground*. And it's always balmy in Huli Huli, which hosts luaus and a full roster of live music events.

Address 26 W Olentangy Street, Powell, OH 43065, +1 (614) 396-8437, www.hulihulipowell.com | **Getting there** By car, take 315 N to OH 750W/E Olentangy Street | **Hours** Tue–Thu 4:30–10pm, Fri 4:30pm–midnight | **Tip** The Kahiki Chapter of the Fraternal Order of Maoi, which celebrates tiki culture, holds a Hot Rod Hula Hop festival each summer to raise funds for children with congenital muscular dystrophy (CMD). Admission is free and there's live entertainment, crafts, and food (www.facebook.com/hotrodhulahop).

50 Insane Asylum Cemeteries
There's more than one?

Several markers erected in 2009 by the State of Ohio, "recognize the courage of past state hospital residents who lived with mental illness and inspired future understanding." One of the markers is at the State of Ohio Asylum for the Insane Cemetery (Broad Street), and another at the adjacent Training Institute of Central Ohio (TICO) cemetery, also known as the Columbus State Hospital Asylum Cemetery. The third marker can be found at the nearby State Old Insane and Penal Cemetery (Harper Road). And the fourth is at the State New Insane Cemetery, also on Broad Street. But it's a bit late for the long-deceased subjects.

The first three cemeteries, well-maintained and located fairly close to one another, are open to the public, with graves dating from the 1840s until the 1970s. The crème de la creepy is the flat stone at the TICO cemetery marked, *Specimen*, which lends itself to speculation: body parts, scientific experimentation…? Also of note are the impersonal stones inscribed with inmates' numbers and an *F* and *M* to designate their gender. Others have only first or last names and dates with a question mark regarding missing information.

But what's truly bizarre is the history of the institutions themselves. Built in 1835, the Lunatic Asylum of Ohio burned down in a mysterious fire some 33 years later. Inmates were shuffled to other institutions until its replacement, the Columbus State Hospital, a sprawling behemoth relocated on the West Side, opened in 1877. The largest building until the Pentagon was built, it was shuttered in the 1980s and eventually razed.

TICO, a juvenile detention center, which also closed in the 1980s, was the subject of investigation by the National Criminal Justice Reference Center for abuse, beatings, rapes, and even disappearance of children who were supposedly released. Some of TICO's survivors are now telling their stories.

Address State of Ohio Asylum for the Insane Cemetery, behind the building at 2130 W Broad Street, Columbus, OH 43223 | Getting there Bus 10 to W Broad Street & S Highland Avenue | Hours Dawn–dusk | Tip Ratchet up the creep factor with an after-dark exploration of an abandoned highway that begins at Scioto Audubon Metro Park, crosses I-70, and goes nowhere, with darkened underpasses, litter, graffiti, and rumors of zombies (400 W Whittier Street, Columbus, OH 43215, www.metroparks.net).

51___J Avenue Japanese Collections

Take a day trip to Tokyo

A visit to the venerated Japanese Marketplace can be likened to an excursion to its namesake or at least to major West Coast cities with a strong Asian presence. The venue comprises Tensuke Market, a full-service grocery store with a casual dining option; Belle's Bread, a Japanese/French bakery; eateries Akai Hana and relative newcomer Sushi 10; and J Avenue, the marketplace opened in the 1980s in the Northwest side. As home base for many workers from Honda and other mid-Ohio-based Japanese companies, the neighborhood became a magnet for even more Asian shops and eateries.

But J Avenue, whose goal is "to embody the…virtue of *omotenashi* – of service beyond service," according to their website, offers a window into the culture far beyond Pokemon, Hello Kitty, and the gazillion Japanese-made *kawaii* tchotchkes, although they have plenty of those as well. Light, airy, and uncluttered, the store personifies *shibui*, the aesthetic of simple, subtle, and unobtrusive beauty.

Beauty products abound. Browsers can discover an incredible variety of hand creams, soap, moisturizers, hair dyes, shampoos, and special cotton balls. You can also find treatment packs for your face, hands, and feet. Those looking for the relaxation of Japanese hot springs can test-drive sample packs of bath salts, including scented, cooling, warming, or spa treatment. Or experiment with the art of growing miniature plants through Shippon, Chuppon, and Eggling products, some of which are self-watering and others that require more maintenance. Adventuresome cooks can try their hand at hard-boiled egg molds in fish, car and other fun shapes, and *onigiri* molds for filled rice balls.

Plus there are enough toys to intrigue even the most restless companion, regardless of age.

Address 1160 Kenny Centre Mall, Columbus, OH 43220, +1 (614) 451-7008, www.javenue.us | **Getting there** Bus 1 to Kenny Road & Folkestone Road | **Hours** Mon–Sat 10am–6pm, Sun 11am–6pm | **Tip** Belle's Bread's unique Japanese-French fusion macaroons, sweet and savory crepes, cake slices and wedding cakes, assorted cream puffs and parfaits have earned local popularity and national recognition (1168 Kenny Centre Mall, Columbus, OH 43220, www.bellesbread.com).

52 Jack Nicklaus Museum
Golden bear necessities

This in-depth look at golf and its superstar is surprisingly engaging, even for those with little interest in the sport. The 24,000-square-foot Jack Nicklaus Museum honors the unparalleled 18 major championships (including six Masters) and over 100 worldwide professional victories of the Columbus native and OSU alum who has earned the moniker of 'Golden Bear'.

Inside, you will find innumerable trophies, exhibit galleries describing the most challenging and historical courses, three theaters illustrating his various accomplishments, culminating in a re-creation of the Bear's man-cave – beige leather couches, blonde wood paneling, portraits of tow-haired offspring and all. Nicklaus' entire life is documented, from his baby shoes to his childhood scrawls to his early wins as a championship athlete in not only golf but tennis and other sports.

Like Elvis, Nicklaus' weight gain and losses are also chronicled, along with his various techniques, putters, and irons, as well as his clothing and hairstyles. His career continued long past any athlete's sell-by date, illustrated by a 46-year-old Nicklaus' age-unprecedented and yet-to-be-bested triumph at the 1986 Masters Tournament. In 1976, he established the Muirfield Memorial Tournament in nearby Dublin, Ohio, which regularly draws luminaries such as Tiger Woods, Fred Couples, and Tom Watson. Unlike Elvis, Nicklaus is still in the building, although infrequently in this one as he's busy designing one of nearly 300 top-of-the-line golf courses in far-flung places like Killeen Castle in Dunsay, Ireland. Or he's in Florida with wife Barbara, 5 children and 22 grandchildren.

Some might say golf is a good walk spoiled, but not at the Jack Nicklaus Museum, where many displays focus on the techniques and nuances of improving your game. Here, everyone can be a winner – especially Nicklaus.

Address 2355 Olentangy River Road, Columbus, OH 43210, +1 (614) 247-5959, www.nicklausmuseum.org | **Getting there** Bus 1 to Olentangy River Road & Argyll Street, walk south on Olentangy, follow signs to Jack Nicklaus Drive | **Hours** Tue – Sat 9am – 5pm | **Tip** Expect inclement weather at the Memorial Tournament. According to local legend, this curse comes courtesy of Chief Leatherlips (see ch. 25), who was executed by his own tribe not far from the site (5750 Memorial Drive, Dublin, OH 43017, www.thememorialtournament.com).

53_Jeffrey Mansion

Parks and recreation for some

Now managed by Bexley Recreation & Parks, Jeffrey Mansion was initially intended as a re-creation of an English estate when it was built in the early 1900s by Columbus native and industrialist Robert Jeffrey and his British-born wife Alice. Jeffrey, the 32nd mayor of Columbus at the time, was not only well-heeled but also well-liked. His mansion was the place to see and be seen.

But a lack of funds hampered its full completion, although the *pièce de résistance*, a "multi-windowed foyer containing a monumental stone stairway," according to a City of Bexley brochure, was finished in 1922 to coincide with a visit from Jeffrey's friend and golfing buddy, President Warren G. Harding. The surrounding 40 acres were populated with trees imported from the UK and Europe, flourishing under the skilled hands of German gardener Herman Carl Kaestner.

Shortly after the Harding visit, however, both Mrs. Jeffrey and Kaestner passed away. Although Jeffrey quickly remarried in 1924, "the Depression, the blight of the Dutch Elm Disease, and the onset of World War II made upkeep of the building and grounds difficult," states the mansion's brochure. So in 1941, Jeffrey donated the mansion to the City of Bexley, "for parks, playgrounds, athletic, recreational, and educational purposes." Neither alcohol nor dogs are permitted, however, and the mansion retains the high-class atmosphere created by its original owners.

The mansion is a favored spot for high school senior pictures, weddings, picnics, and birthday parties, and the grounds are ideal for hikes and nature walks. There's also purportedly a ghost who whistles and messes with the copier in the Recreation & Parks offices on the second floor, adding yet another layer of legend.

Recently, the city passed an ordinance allowing alcohol on the grounds with stringent restrictions. Dogs and panhandlers, however, are still prohibited.

Address 165 N Parkview Avenue, Bexley, OH 43209, +1 (614) 559-4300, www.bexley.org |
Getting there Bus 10 to E Broad Street & S Parkview Avenue, turn right onto N Parkview,
about a 0.3-mile walk | Hours See website for event schedule | Tip Along with a scenic
walking trail that borders Alum Creek, the adjacent 40-acre Jeffrey Park (which shares an
address with the mansion) offers a play area for children, tennis courts, a community pool,
and even kayaking (165 N Parkview Avenue, Bexley, OH 43209, www.bexley.org).

54 Jolly King Gambrinus
The patron saint of beer

Prominently displayed in an enclosed mini-park in the Brewery District, the 11-foot-tall statue of Jolly King Gambrinus appears to be hoisting a soft-serve ice cream cone. But no, it's actually a stein of foaming beer, as testified by not only the hefty belly of the purported inventor of beer himself, but also the fact that his foot is resting on a keg. Like his namesake, the statue has had quite the vagabond provenance. No wonder his expression seems slightly muddled.

By the late 19th century, breweries had become exceedingly popular in the US, with Jolly King Gambrinus being a logical spokessaint/king. Columbus was no exception. Brewer August Wagner, an immigrant from Bavaria, placed the unpainted statue at the entrance of his new Gambrinus Brewery in 1906, where it remained for several decades, through Prohibition and a subsequent business pivot, and when the business returned to brewing as the August Wagner Brewery until closing in 1974. The statue remained, although it was eventually painted and moved when *The Columbus Dispatch* purchased the land, and again in the 2000s to the Brewery District.

As the legend of King Gambrinus goes, he was a European fiddler, who lived around 800 AD Suicidal over a breakup, he was approached by Satan himself, who offered to help him invent beer in exchange for his soul. But when the Devil sent a minion to collect on the debt some 30 years later, Gambrinus got said minion so drunk that he forgot to complete the task. Gambrinus lived to be 100, when he allegedly turned into a beer barrel. It's not the worst fate imaginable. Another origin story is that he could have been one of several Burgundy royals: the ancient King Gampar (aka Gambrivius), John the Fearless (1371–1419), or John I, Duke of Brabant (c. 1252–1294).

Raise a glass in honor of Jolly King Gambrinus every April 11th, his annual holiday.

Address Half a block north of S Front and W Sycamore Streets, Columbus, OH 43201 |
Getting there Bus 5, 8, or 61 to S High, W Sycamore, & S Front Streets | Hours
Unrestricted | Tip Another Brewery District icon in restaurant form is what is now known
as Brick (formerly Handke's), where you can dine in a brewery cellar dating back to the
1800s (520 S Front Street, Columbus, OH 43215, www.brickamericankitchen.com).

55 Jubilee Museum

Funhouse of liturgical treasures

Located in a humble building off a grimy side street is the largest diversified collection of Catholic art in the US, according to the Vatican itself. Worth millions of dollars, the collection is housed in a hodgepodge of rooms inside recycled display cases. Makeup-wearing, stylishly posed mannequins provide incongruous models for an exhibit of nun's habits. The Synagogue Room boasts an ancient ark amid Holocaust-related sculptures. A relic case offers up hundreds of relics – hair, bone fragments, and other artifacts going back to the time of Christ. There are accumulations of altars, colorful vestments, stained-glass windows, Bibles, and so much more.

Father Kevin Lutz founded the museum in 1998. It's hardly glitzy in appearance. The Holy Family Soup Kitchen is located downstairs, and the museum's unassuming reception area, which serves as a temporary warehouse for rotating and seasonal exhibits, has the air of a well-organized garage sale. But once the guided tour is underway, it's a breathtaking – and sometimes amusing – rollercoaster of the opulence and rituals that make up the traditional Catholic Church. Who knew that the Pope's white cap was first cousin to the Jewish yarmulke?

"The museum came in response to a call by the Church that local parishes do something to celebrate the Jubilee year 2000," says Marketing Director Patrick Folley.

An avid collector himself, Lutz transferred his personal collection to the present building, which he also owned. And in that same spirit, the museum grew from 4 rooms to 24, from private donations and also churches that closed. Conversely, the museum will supply a church in need of, say, an altar or nativity scene.

"We're in the process of continually refining exhibits and ramping up our social media presence," adds Folley. So while displays come from centuries past, this museum has quite a future.

Address 57 S Grubb Street, Columbus, OH 43215, +1 (614) 600-0054,
www.jubileemuseum.org, info@jubileemuseum.org | Getting there Bus 3, 6 or 9 to W Rich
Street & S Skidmore Street | Hours Tue–Sat 10am–4pm, Sun 1–4pm | Tip Make your
own Catholic acquisitions of rosaries, scapulars, statues, and books at Generations Religious
Gifts (1095 Dublin Road, Columbus, OH 43215, www.generationsreligiousgifts.com).

56 Juniper Restaurant

From eyesore to showstopper

Built in 1929, with its own rooftop water tower and *Smith Bros' Hardware Co* emblazoned across the front, what was once a humble manufacturing concern is now among the city's hottest restaurants and event spaces. Back in the day, 10-foot reinforced concrete floors and huge windows were meant for heavyweight hardware parts instead of hipsters. Who knew that immediate access to the railroad line for shipping would also provide unparalleled, panoramic views of the downtown skyline?

By 1995, however, the building was headed for the wrecking ball, due to a two-alarm fire the year before. Shuttered in the 1980s, it had fallen into disrepair, a hangout for skateboarders and the homeless. Juniper's owner, Steve Rayo, recognized good bones, and within a few years it was transformed into cool, loft-style offices. It also helped that its centralized Italian Village location was being revitalized.

Juniper is the proverbial icing, a 12,000-square-foot rooftop greenhouse where humans can flourish. Summers represent a completely outdoor experience, while inclement weather can provide a cozy, snow globe feel, thanks in part to heated floors.

Along with a fully retractable ceiling and walls and clear chairs so as not to obstruct the view, the speakeasy-meets-Gatsby art deco décor includes mosaic tiles, geometric prints, and a mirrored bar with a railroad-tie bar footrest. Lounge-style clusters encourage private gathering amid a minimalist, open setting. An open-style trough for hand washing before entering separate men's and women's restrooms is an edgy touch.

The Caribbean-American menu ranges from flatbreads to chickpea cakes to a hearty New York strip steak. But most people are there for atmosphere anyway. Would you like to live full-time with an industrial ambiance? Rent a loft at the former Wonder Bread factory a couple of blocks away.

Address 580 N 4th Street, Columbus, OH 43215, +1 (614) 464-3333, www.juniperrooftop.com, info@juniperrooftop.com | Getting there Bus 1, 2, or 5 to N High & Spruce Streets, 0.4-mile walk, right on Goodale, left on 4th Street | Hours Tue–Thu 5–10:30pm, Fri 5pm–midnight, Sun 11am–2:30pm | Tip Since 1876, the nearby North Market has offered everything from fresh fish to gourmet ice cream (59 Spruce Street, Columbus, OH 43215, www.northmarket.com).

57 Jurassic Journey Exhibit
Hole-in-one excavation

Imagine you are part of a work crew digging a water feature at the Burning Tree Golf Course, when your shovel hits some large bones. And it's not just any skeleton – it is the most complete mastodon ever found in the US, preserved for some 12,000 years after early humans likely drove the beast into a cold peat bog, where they killed it with spears. Preserved in the peat, the animal's bones, muscle, and cartilage also revealed bacteria in the stomach, including eight species thought to be extinct. Declared one of the 50 most significant scientific findings of the decade, the 'Burning Tree Mastodon,' named after the golf course, was sold to a Japanese museum for $600,000. But not before the course's owner, Sherm Byers, made a replica for himself.

The discovery took place in 1989, but the fully assembled copy consisting of some 150 bones can be found today at the Jurassic Journey exhibit at the course, along with an 11-foot-tall, 15-foot-long super-dino, created from latex foam and spray painted with dark colors. You'll also see fiberglass reproductions of a *Tyrannosaurus rex*, brontosaurus, stegosaurus, velociraptor, and others in a 3,000-square-foot, garage-like space.

And for the right price, you can probably buy one or more of the critters in stock and take it home. For many years, with an assist from paleontologist Joe Taylor, Byers ran quite the cottage industry, creating copies of the mastodon skeleton and other dinos for Walt Disney, Ripley's Believe It or Not, and overseas museums. During the 1990s, he also set up displays at the Ohio State Fair as well as traveling educational exhibits.

But if you have to ask, you may not be able to afford it. Depending on the size and complexity of the reproduction, these creatures can cost tens of tens of thousands of dollars. Although Byers and company are no longer making them, their dinosaurs live on.

Address 4600 Ridgely Tract Road SE, Newark, OH 43056, +1 (740) 522-3464, www.burningtreegc.com/jurassic-journey-exhibit | Getting there By car, take 161E/37E/16E, turn right on River Road, turn right onto Thornwood Drive SW, then left onto Ridgely Tract Road SE | Hours By appointment only | Tip Want more 'saurs? The huge AMNH Dinosaur Gallery at the Center of Science and Industry (COSI) consists of more reproductions, artifacts, and evolutionary information than you can shake an 8-foot-long femur at (333 W Broad Street, Columbus, OH 43215, www.cosi.org/exhibits/dinos).

58__Jury Room

Serving more than justice since 1831

"Serving more than justice since 1831," is the slogan of the Jury Room Bar, Ohio's purported oldest bar, located across from the Franklin County Courthouse. The bar has operated under many names: Blind Lady Tavern, Irvin's Place, J.F. Gaiser Saloon and Boarding House, and the noir-ish Wine and Bar. Decades of lawyering up, wheeling, dealing, and propositioning – in all senses of the word – have become ingrained into the very floorboards. The interior remains classy though, with a gleaming wood bar, tin ceiling, and Victorian-style chandelier.

The land, supposedly the former site of an Indian burial ground, was originally given as payment to soldier Thomas Asbury for his service during the American Revolution. The building was originally three stories high until a fire in the 1870s destroyed the top floor.

Now an event space, the Jury Room was also a boarding house and brothel, where, according to *Historic Columbus Taverns,* Union officers were hosted one night and high-ranking Confederates from nearby Camp Chase prison the next. In 1858, Frances Miller, the bordello's madam, shot and killed a young man, Paulus Rupprecht, as he and a bunch of his randy friends tried to enter after hours. Miller spent 11 years in prison for manslaughter and upon her release, was allegedly never able to get back on her feet again. Her ghost is purported to haunt the place, and at one time, the waitstaff kept a log of sightings and odd occurrences, including piano music, mysterious figures, and the inevitable knocking over of barstools and glasses. The basement was used for ghost tours and was featured on the Travel Channel's, *The Dead Files.*

The current owners, Mark and Megan Dempsey, have big plans for the tavern, including renting out office space and using an upstairs apartment as an Airbnb, especially convenient for potential wedding parties. Ghosts included.

Address 22 E Mound Street, Columbus, OH 43215, +1 (614) 869-0040, www.thejuryroomcolumbus.com, juryroomcolumbus@gmail.com | **Getting there** Bus 7 to E Main Street & S High Street | **Hours** By appointment only | **Tip** Get some righteous good eats at the nearby Zagat-rated Pearl, which offers creative American fare, along with an oyster bar and specialty drinks (641 N High Street, Columbus, OH 43215, www.thepearlcolumbus.com).

59 Kelton House Museum & Garden

Well-mannered history

Kelton House Museum & Garden, a community service of the Junior League of Columbus, was built in 1852 by Fernando and Sophia Kelton. It hits the sweet spot between respectability and political correctness. It is the site of programs and tours and Victorian teas and serves as a popular wedding venue. Outfitted with heavy wood furniture, glowing chandeliers, chintz wall coverings, and ornate place settings, it was also a rather unconventional stop on the Underground Railroad.

The Kelton family deliberately built their home far away from the city so as to coordinate activities with their fellow Abolitionists and help escaped slaves to pass through unnoticed. Ten-year-old Martha Hartway was so ill that the Keltons took her in. She stayed while her sister traveled on to Wisconsin. Martha eventually married cabinetmaker Thomas Lawrence, a free Black man who worked for the Keltons. This story would have been lost over time, except that, in the 1970s, the wife of Lawrence's grandson found a handful of photos and asked her husband, "Who are these white people?" They contacted Sophia's granddaughter Grace who still lived at the residence, and Martha's story became part of Kelton House lore.

Fernando Kelton, a merchant, was selected to be a Columbus pallbearer in President Lincoln's burial procession. Kelton's son Frank married one of the first four women to attend Ohio State University. Grace Kelton, who remained single, was one of the first professional interior designers.

And while the ghosts of the family are still said to be playing innocent pranks and moving things around in their home, they are not above reprimanding the occasional rude visitor during the docent-led tours, such as hitting two non-stop talkers in the rear end with a cabinet door.

Address 586 E Town Street, Columbus, OH 43215, +1 (614) 464-2022,
www.kcltonhouse.com | Getting there Bus 11 to E Town Street & Lester Drive |
Hours Tue–Fri 10am–4pm, Sat & Sun 1–4pm | Tip Built in 1811, the Orange
Johnson House offers an even earlier glimpse of Ohio's pioneer and Federal eras
with rotating exhibits and some original artifacts (956 High Street, Worthington,
OH 43085, www.worthingtonhistory.org).

60__King Arts Complex
Colorblind education and entertainment

About half of the people who walk through the doors of the King Arts Complex aren't Black. And any thoughts of skin color are immediately wiped out by a 6 × 6-foot portrait of Dr. Martin Luther King Jr. himself near the entrance. The brainchild of artist Franz Spohn, the work is made entirely with gumballs and was constructed in 2012 with the assistance of local schoolchildren. The lines of balls are encased entirely in plastic, which makes them unavailable for sampling, no matter how tempting.

There is a claustrophobic re-creation of a Middle Passage slave trade ship replete with vivid murals accompanied by leg irons and chains. An 18th-century African slave castle and Jim Crow 'Whites Only' restroom sign serve as other uncomfortable and chilling reminders. The complex, however, is about more than race. The true focus is on the arts community and the triumph of the human spirit.

The work and memorabilia of folk artist Minah Robinson, photographer Kojo Kamau, singer Nancy Wilson, organist Hank Marr, and other greater and lesser knowns are showcased. The Elijah Pierce Gallery, named after the legendary woodcarver, features rotating exhibits, including the artistic endeavors of local youngsters. Regularly scheduled programming ranges from school tours to 'First Tuesday' teas for seniors to a summer Jazz Heritage program to a formal annual gala, and much more.

In 1987, when the complex opened in the newly renovated 1920s Pythian Temple, where legendary musicians Duke Ellington and others performed, the community got behind it in a big way, raising $2.7 million through city, state, and corporate contributions. Two years later, it expanded again, with acquisition of an adjacent elementary school, doubling in size to 60,000 square feet.

Along with injecting new life into a grand dame and the surrounding area, the King Arts Complex warms the hearts of all who enter.

Address 867 Mount Vernon Avenue, Columbus, OH 43203, +1 (614) 645-5464,
kingartscomplex.com, info@kingartscomplex.com | Getting there Bus 7 to Mount Vernon
& N Garfield Avenues | Hours Mon–Fri 9am–6pm, Sat 11am–3pm | Tip Continue your
cultural journey into the cooking arts at Madison Soul Food Kitchen. Located in the United
House of Prayer Church, this cafeteria-style operation serves up homemade vittles ranging
from pork chops to fried chicken, with sides like greens and mashed potatoes with gravy
(1731 Greenway Avenue, Columbus, OH 43203).

61_Kingmakers
Serious fun and games, the perfect pairing

What has 500 titles, costs $5 to enter, and is curated by sommeliers? That would be Kingmakers, the board game parlor. Step away from all of your screens for a few hours of fun with friends in actual 'meat space.' Don't knock it until you try it.

There's something here for every inclination, including options for groups of two to large parties. Super competitive types can choose Codenames, Decrypto, or Taboo. Or opt for a game of deception, like Secret Hitler, Bang, and Ghost Blitz. Mysterium is perfect for visually oriented players. The full gamut of classics spans the lesser-known Ticket to Ride and Carcassonne, to the tried and true Monopoly and Chutes and Ladders. Basic checkers and chess boards, and even ancient cribbage are there too. Cat lovers can explore nine lives through Cat Lady and Exploding Kittens, while the more curious options include Cockroach Clicker, Crappy Birthday, and Obama Llama. The darker side is chronicled via Army of Darkness and Zombicide. Board game sommeliers, staff members who can match games with gamers' personal preferences and tastes, will help you find the perfect pairing.

The brainchild of Malika de Silva and Rebekah Sherman, who met while working in a restaurant, opened Kingmakers in Columbus in 2014, with another venue in Indianapolis three years later. After investigating Snakes and Lattes, a similar enterprise in Toronto, de Silva decided to try her luck here. Fans have been ready to play games here ever since.

The main focus of Kingmakers is to bring people together through playing board games, although you can enjoy draft beer, wine, and even mead, and there's also an intriguing selection of specialty sodas as well as an eclectic snack menu. So settle in on a table with friends, acquaintances and even strangers for a night of good, usually clean and potentially raucous fun.

Address 17 Buttles Avenue, Columbus, OH 43215, +1 (614) 643-0785, www.kingmakersfun.com | **Getting there** Bus 1 to N High Street & Buttles Avenue | **Hours** Tue–Thu 5–11pm, Fri 5pm–1am, Sat & Sun 1pm–1am | **Tip** More nonalcoholic socialization can be found at Eat Purr Love Cat Café, where your take-home fare may involve a cat carrier for one of the adoptable resident felines (3041 Indianola Avenue, Columbus, OH 43202, www.eatpurrlovecatcafe.com).

62 Krema Nut Company
Nut nirvana

Since 1898, Krema Nut Company has been churning out peanut butter, at first for senior citizens as an easily ingested form of protein, then later for kids of all ages. The oldest peanut butter manufacturer in the US, Krema has endured throughout the decades, at one point splitting into two separate enterprises, although the Krema manufacturing plant, located in Plain City, was renamed Crazy Richard's in 2016, to prevent driving customers nuts with confusion.

The Columbus-based enterprise still makes and sells *au natural* (no salt, sugar, or preservatives) nut butters under the Krema label. But the creamy, crunchy, hot and spicy peanut options, along with almond, pistachio, and cashew butters, are but a kernel of their over 200 offerings. Along with a huge selection of bagged nuts, they purvey jelly, flavored popcorns, chocolates and candies, mixed snacks, dried fruits, and even a sugar-free line of goodies. While these, along with a selection of T-shirts ("The Finest Nuts Since 1898"), can be purchased online, the real fun is in visiting the actual physical location, which offers shelf after shelf of mind-boggling options for every taste bud.

While at the store, you can also partake of their snack bar, which serves up gourmet peanut butter and jelly sandwiches, ranging from the all-American Grandma's Apple Pie (peanut butter topped with chunky apple fruit spread) to the eye-watering Kicker (hot & spicy peanut butter topped with piquant raspberry preserves), to the inevitable Buckeye (ground peanut butter with chocolate hazelnut spread). As if that's not enough calories and fat, ice cream cones, gooey sundaes, and thick peanut butter-flavored milkshakes are available for dessert.

Factory tours are no longer offered, likely because of allergy and insurance concerns. But the heavenly smell of roasted nuts and free samples should more than compensate.

Address 1000 Goodale Boulevard, Columbus, OH 43212, +1 (614) 299-4131, www.krema.com, nuts@krema.com | Getting there Bus 3 to 868 W Goodale Boulevard, walk west about 0.2 miles | Hours Mon–Fri 9am–5pm, Sat 9am–2pm | Tip Work off the calories at the 120-acre Scioto Audubon Metro Park, which offers hiking, biking, water sports, and a climbing wall with scenic riverside views (400 W Whittier Street, Columbus, OH 43215, www.metroparks.net).

63 __ The Last York Steak House
Flavors of the past

Step into York Steak House, and it hits you like big hair, shoulder pads, and Cabbage Patch kids: you're back in the 1980s. Between the darkish, medieval castle interior with its iron chandeliers and heavy wood paneling, and the giant slab menu board with pictures of various offerings – make up your mind now or forever hold your peace – the last remaining York Steak House is the restaurant that time forgot.

Founded in 1966 by Columbus residents Berndt Gros and Eddie Grayson, who were inspired by the success of Ponderosa (York's salad bar is a nod to that heritage), according to *Columbus Monthly*, "The two planned details of the experience, from yelling orders to the line chef in French (it's more exotic) to placing desserts in the front of the line (before customers' trays filled up with other choices) to ensure that the booths had rounded corners (so people wouldn't hurt themselves when getting up)." Their growth strategy of opening near shopping malls proved so successful that a decade later, they were bought out by General Mills (later called Darden) Restaurant Group. By the early 1990s, however, food courts and the closing of many malls signed the death warrant for the nearly 180 York franchisees.

Privately owned by Jay Bettin, who started working there in the 1980s, this lone remaining York is a destination unto itself. The clientele mostly consists of regulars, refugees from the nearby Hollywood Casino, and nostalgia fans making the pilgrimage from distant parts for that unique and still relatively inexpensive flavor fix of grilled steak and sirloin, honey-glazed chicken, chocolate pudding, and fluffy rolls. Either Bettin himself or a friendly server bustles about, refilling drinks and chatting up the customers.

York Steak House is not fancy, and it's certainly old-school. Alcohol is neither served nor offered. But that's beside the point.

Address 4220 W Broad Street, Columbus, OH 43228, +1 (614) 272-6485, www.york-steakhouse.com, yorksteakhouseohio@gmail.com | Getting there Bus 10 to 4250 W Broad Street | Hours Mon–Thu 11am–8:30pm, Fri & Sat 11am–9pm, Sun 11am–8:30pm | Tip Gamble away the money you saved by eating at York on some 2,200 slots, 70 table games, and a huge poker room at the nearby Hollywood Casino (200 Georgesville Road, Columbus, OH 43228, www.hollywoodcolumbus.com).

64 Lincoln Theatre

A true Egyptian revival

Once the crown jewel of Columbus' largely Black King-Lincoln District, the Lincoln Theatre was slated for demolition in the early 1990s. Opened in 1928 by two entrepreneurs in response to a nearby 'no admission to negroes' theater, what was initially the Ogden Theatre and Ballroom quickly became the community's place to see and be seen. The sumptuous, gilded Egyptian Revival décor was not only completely African-American built, owned, and operated but boasted massive, ornate stage pillars, an Isis symbol above the proscenium, and Temple of Karnak-inspired touches everywhere, including the seats.

Renamed the Lincoln in 1939, it offered the latest in films, vaudeville shows, and its specialty, jazz. A three-year-old Sammy Davis Jr. made his stage debut there. Count Basie, Duke Ellington, Etta James, and many others graced the second-floor jazz ballroom that rivaled Harlem renaissance nightclubs.

The construction of a major highway in the late 1960s and early 1970s separated the King-Lincoln District from downtown, displacing 10,000 residents and effectively signing the death warrant for many businesses there. Integration, migration to the suburbs, and the growing use of autos also contributed to the Lincoln's early 1970s demise.

However, rescue came in the form of exterior repairs and its 1992 addition to the National Register of Historic Places. Revival shifted into high gear in 2000 when then Mayor Michael Coleman announced plans to revitalize the entire district. The city purchased the theater property and enlisted the Columbus Association for the Performing Arts to spearhead the $13-million renovation. The entire community rallied around the cause, culminating in a 2009 grand reopening.

Today, the Lincoln is a cutting-edge hub for visual, written, and performance arts. Regardless of race, creed, or color, everyone is welcome.

Address 769 E Long Street, Columbus, OH 43203, +1 (614) 719-6746, www.lincolntheatrecolumbus.com | **Getting there** Bus 11 to E Long Street & Talmadge Street | **Hours** See website for schedule | **Tip** Enjoy more cool jazz on Saturday nights across the street at the Lincoln Café. The service is friendly and the atmosphere ideal for pre/post-performance coffee or a cocktail (740 E Long Street, www.lincolncafecols.com).

65 __ Local 67 Pagoda
The fancy firehouse

You're driving down W Broad Street, admiring the revitalization of the surrounding Franklinton area and shiny new downtown buildings, and there it is: a three-story, red brick pagoda. Even weirder, the structure, which began life in 1895 as a railroad station, is now home to Local 67, the Columbus Firefighters Union.

Actually intended to be a combination of French and Swiss feudal architecture, the structure was initially fronted by a large clock on the tower, which served as a timekeeper for passers-by. The clock has long since been removed, and the railroad tracks, originally at ground level, were elevated in 1910 to accommodate the growing number of horseless carriages, adding to the Asian flair. It's amazing that the Pagoda, as it's still informally called, even survived at all. Two devastating fires, one in 1910 and another 65 years later, burned off the roof, and floods in 1913 and 1959 caused considerable damage. The Volunteers of America (VOA), who took it over in 1930, did some refurbishing of the barrel-shaped lobby, the ticket window, and the cherubs on the ceiling. But for many years, the Pagoda was marginally skid row, due to its location and the VOA's clientele.

Enter the Firefighter's Union, which snapped up the vacated property in 2006. In true first responder fashion, they installed a sprinkler system and renovated the building inside and out, spiffing up and repairing the drafty interior while maintaining the elegant Victorian woodwork on the ceiling and elsewhere. They even added a meeting hall and park, and they rent out the space for weddings, bar/bat mitzvahs and bachelorette parties, although the firefighters themselves are not available for entertainment. Trains still rumble by several times during the day, shaking everything accordingly.

But you don't need a special occasion to stop by and enjoy the view…and pick up some firefighter swag at the gift kiosk.

Address 379 W Broad Street, Columbus, OH 43215, +1 (614) 481-8900 | Getting there Bus 10 or 12 to W Broad Street & Belle Street | Hours Mon–Fri 7am–3pm | Tip Along with basic Italian food, the Spaghetti Warehouse next door serves up its own brand of railroad memorabilia, including a bright red refurbished rail car where you can dine, as well as other turn-of-the-20th-century touches (397 W Broad Street, Columbus, OH 43215, www.meatballs.com).

66___Longview Barber Shop

Shaving and haircutting for over a century

The last thing on barber Tom Pletcher's mind when he returned from WWI was opening his own shop. But his job at his hometown in Zanesville had been filled, so he moved to Clintonville, where his sister lived, renting a room in a nearby pharmacy, then relocated to the corner of Longview and High Streets. He opened the Longview Barber Shop, which has since been through seven owners, several wars, and countless changes in hairstyles.

The secret to Clintonville's oldest traditional yet trendy business is simple. Do the job right and know when to keep quiet. Hair salons are notorious for attracting gossip; the mere act of trimming locks invites intimacy. So when a regular customer comes, asks for a cut that's short in front and longish in back, "the barber knows that he wants a mullet but doesn't call it that," explains current owner Dave Carty. Thus, the often-ridiculed 'man bun' is referred to as an 'undercut.'

Yet despite its funky, almost thrown-together décor – a waiting area with what looks like recycled theater seats, a ratty old barber stool with a half-mannequin advertising the shop's T-shirts, and photos and memorabilia spanning decades – the place is definitely on-trend. Professional men and women barbers of all styles and orientations snip a clientele that is just as varied. Yet haircutters have their specialties. "No one is shy about referring a customer to another barber," says Carty.

Carty also attributes Longview's longevity to a bit of luck. "During the 1960s and 1970s when long hair was popular, we were saved by nearby parochial schools that required regulation cuts for male students." More recently, Carty continues, "The Internet has raised our profile and brought in new customers."

Generations of families keep coming back too. "There's nothing like seeing a customer who got his first haircut here take their kids in for theirs."

Address 3325 N High Street, Columbus, OH 43202, +1 (614) 268-0885,
www.longviewbarbershop.com, longviewbarbershop@yahoo.com | Getting there Bus 102 to
N High Street & F. North Broadway | Hours Mon – Fri 9am – 5:30pm, Sat 8am – 2pm | Tip
A quiet respite can be found a few blocks away at Walhalla Ravine, a tucked-away gorge
with beautiful views, a spring, and wildlife (Walhalla Road, Columbus, OH 43202).

67 Lustron Homes
Fab prefab houses

Located at the nonprofit Ohio History Connection is a 1950s time capsule: a two-bedroom, 1,085-square-foot, dove gray West Chester Deluxe Lustron Home. Inside, a boy's room is decked-out with a cowboy print bedspread and matching curtains. The small kitchen is dotted with vintage appliances, recipe boxes, and cookbooks. Pictures and other decorative touches hang from the walls with magnets, eliminating the need for those pesky nail holes. The dining area has built-in porcelain and enamel cabinets and a chrome-accented table for a family of four. One of only about 2,500 homes built by the Lustron Corporation between 1948 and 1950, this example serves as a reminder that even if things are done right, they can still go very wrong.

In 1947, Columbus businessman Carl Strandlund got it in his head to mass-produce porcelain enameled steel panels originally used to build gas stations. Designed to accommodate returning GIs and their burgeoning families, the prefabricated homes, to be assembled on-site, were maintenance-free, with built-ins and pocket doors, and were easy to clean. They came blue-green, green, pink, and white and retained their colors for many years. Some models even offered the 'Automagic,' a combo dishwasher-washing machine. All starting at the low price of $4,200!

Strandlund got the government's buy-in for an unprecedented $15.5 million loan. But Lustron quickly ran into production problems, which more than doubled the average cost. Demand exceeded supply, resulting in backorders. Conflicting building codes, complications in obtaining financing, unpaid loans, and Congressional opposition to a government-subsidized operation all contributed to its bankruptcy. By 1951, Lustron had closed its doors.

Today Lustron Homes still serve their original purpose at these private addresses: 272 E Weisheimer Road, 27 Kanawha Avenue, 214 Arden Road, and 185 Arden Road.

Address Ohio History Connection, 800 E 17th Avenue, Columbus, OH 43211,
+1 (614) 297-2300, www.ohiohistory.org | Getting there Bus 8 to McGuffey Road &
Duxberry Avenue or to Hamilton Avenue & E 17th Avenue, walk west on 17th Avenue |
Hours Wed–Sun 10am–5pm | Tip For a different kind of prefab home, the nearby
Korbel North Campground is a great place to park your camper during the Ohio State
Fair (717 E 17th Avenue, Columbus, OH 43211, www.ohiostatefair.com/camping).

68 ModCon Living Tool Library

Handy Dandy

According to The World Record Academy Hall of Fame, the world's first tool lending library was started in Columbus in 1976. We're talking hammers, saws, ladders, drills, paintbrushes, lawn mowers, screwdrivers, shovels, and many more. Over 4,000 tools and pieces of equipment are available to both individuals and nonprofit organizations in Franklin County for a nominal membership fee, reduced even more for low-income individuals. So whether it's for metalworking, carpentry, electrical, plumbing, remodeling, or maintenance for your car, bike, house, or garden, they've got you covered. To this end, most of the tools are pretty standard, although some of the unusual exceptions include a vintage nail puller, a long metal bar with an odd-looking clamp, and a five-foot-long homemade bush uprooter with giant tongs. Members must return the tools, undamaged, within the allotted time or face strict fines, just like with books, but louder.

Like some of its clientele, the library has seen challenging times. Founded by the City of Columbus using federal funds, it was initially free to all Columbus residents. However, when funds dried up due to the recession, the library was taken over in 2009 by the nonprofit home-repair group today known as ModCon Living. Along with initiating the Tool Library Membership Program, ModCon also provides grant-funded home repair services to low-income senior and disabled homeowners, as well as maintaining a database of reasonably-priced repair personnel for the risk-averse who'd rather leave it to a professional. They engage the general population through regular fundraisers and volunteer efforts to help disadvantaged homeowners.

While tool libraries are catching on in other cities thanks to the trend toward sharing goods and services, ModCon Living has been at the forefront for the community.

Address 2771 E 4th Avenue, Columbus, OH 43219, +1 (614) 258-6392, www.modconliving.org/tool-library | **Getting there** Bus 7 to E 5th Avenue & Alton Avenue | **Hours** Members only, and tours are available by appointment | **Tip** Some public libraries, such as Worthington's, also lend air-quality monitors, auto-code readers, car jump-starters, and camping tents and gear. All you need is your library card (various locations, www.worthingtonlibraries.org).

69___Motorcycle Hall of Fame
Generations of easy riders

Motorcycles go as far back as 1885, when German inventor Gottlieb Daimler built the first 'motorized bicycle,' or a bicycle with an engine between its wheels. A rare reproduction of what's known as the Daimler Reitwagen ("Riding Wagon") can be found in the American Motorcyclist Association Motorcycle Hall of Fame. Interestingly, this early motorcycle bears an "everything old is new again" resemblance to today's electric bicycles that have recently become so popular.

The museum also has early model Indians and Harleys, as well as sleek rides from famous racers, including Wayne Rainey's Kawasaki GPz750 air-cooled superbike and Doug Henry's pioneering motocross YZM400. There are hundreds of BMWs, Harley-Davidsons, and Hondas, along with lesser-known brands.

The AMA preceded the Hell's Angels by several decades. Founded in 1924, it was organized to protect riders' rights and serve the industry. Although the museum/hall of fame, established by the nonprofit American Motorcycle Heritage Foundation (AMHF), opened its doors in 1990, the collection soon outgrew the space and in 1999 was moved to the 23-acre AMA headquarters in Pickerington, almost doubling in size to 26,000 square feet.

Past exhibits have included custom choppers, history of motorcycle clubs, and women and motorcycles. The museum also serves up what its website calls "the greatest collection of motorcycle sidecar toys known to man" and a "Birth of a Hurricane" display honoring engineer Craig Vetter, who helped the Brits design and market the now obscure Triumph Hurricane in the early 1970s. The Hall of Fame honors both the high-profile speed racers and lesser knowns, such as 2018 inductee Mary McGee, one of the first women in the US to race motorcycles in motocross and other events.

Gearheads will appreciate the design and engineering, and others will dream of the open road.

Address 13515 Yarmouth Drive, Pickerington, OH 43147, +1 (614) 856-2222, www.motorcyclemuseum.org, info@motorcyclemuseum.org | **Getting there** By car, take I-70 E to OH-256 E/Baltimore-Reynoldsburg Road/Hill Road N in Pickerington, left on Blacklick-Eastern Road NW, then left on Yarmouth Drive | **Hours** Daily 9am–5pm | **Tip** More funky bikes and cars can be found at the Picktown Palooza, an annual, three-day summer carnival that features food, rides, entertainment, and a family-friendly 5k run (www.picktownpalooza.org).

70 Motts Military Museum
War toys

What do you do with, say, the Bible that took a bullet for you during the Vietnam War? Or Saddam Hussein's confiscated china and silverware? Or the Civil War amputation kit handed down from great-grandfather? Put it in Motts Military Museum to be seen and remembered.

A professional photographer by trade and war memorabilia collector by hobby, army veteran and owner/curator Warren Motts opened his museum in 1987 in his family home, moving a few years later to a nearby 5,100-square-foot facility on nearly four acres of land. Soon, that filled up too, as veterans and their families from around the world began to hear about the museum and donate vehicles, military aircraft, even a Higgins Boat from WWII, among thousands of other items. The museum has expanded several times since then, adding a new wing in 2015 and a faithful reproduction of aviator Eddie Rickenbacker's childhood home.

Built and supported solely by volunteers, private donors, and the Motts family, this museum rivals any professionally curated collection. Exhibits are arranged by conflict, starting with the Revolutionary War through Operation Iraqi Freedom, along with displays highlighting NASA, POWs, and the Tuskegee Airmen, among others. Plan on spending several hours wandering among the well-lit and carefully preserved objects. The WWII collection alone has blood-stained maps, uniforms, and family portraits of Nazi officers. Mussolini's flag, a wedding dress made from a parachute, and artifacts from the Holocaust. Along with a recently opened memorial garden to honor veterans and active duty personnel, the museum is developing a huge 9/11 exhibit, to include FDNY Ladder 18, a fire truck that was crushed during the 2001 collapse of the World Trade Center.

Although war makes fascinating history, this museum both honors war and serves as a cautionary tale.

Address 5075 S Hamilton Road, Groveport, OH 43125, +1 (614) 836-1500, www.mottsmilitarymuseum.org, info@mottsmilitarymuseum.org | Getting there By car, take I-70 E to US-33 E, to OH-317 S Hamilton Road and turn right, drive about two miles | Hours Tue–Sat 9am–5pm, Sun 1–5pm | Tip In addition to touring the outside, which has been refurbished and has markers with historical information, visitors can also go into Rickenbacker's actual childhood home, which had previously been closed to the public (1334 E Livingston Avenue, Columbus, OH 43205, www.facebook.com/RWFLC).

71__Mystic Nirvana

Staying in good spirits

Located in the ironically named Stoner Building – among mid-1800s Westerville burgher George Stoner's several developed properties, it was headquarters for the National Anti-Saloon League – Mystic Nirvana is both medium and large. Well-known local psychic Brenda Posani is the former, and her shop is the latter, with an ample selection of books, art, jewelry, and healing totems that will appeal to believers and non-believers alike.

The building is also allegedly haunted, according to Posani, who has seen, photographed, and recorded phenomena there, including shadow figures on the porch, a white light going in and out of the building, a woman dressed in 1850s clothing, and others. Like Casper, most are considered friendly ghosts.

A native of Kentucky, Posani started her enterprise in her home, doing readings, teaching classes on meditation and psychometry (the ability to learn facts about an event or person by touching inanimate objects), and blessings or clearings of businesses and homes with paranormal activities. All for a fee of course. Along with some predictions that apparently became true, she's regularly featured in local media and as a speaker. She is also a genial and approachable shopkeeper, more like the lady next door than a long-taloned tarot reader with a crystal ball. Her energy sits especially well with newbies who may be nervous about seeing a psychic, "I am not a negative reader. However, I do state what I feel," she says. "We all have free will."

She opened Mystic Nirvana in 2009 and changed addresses a couple of times, recently settling on the current location, which was Stoner's actual home. Along with being Native American ritual grounds, the current spot has been a station on the Underground Railroad, a spa, and a physician's office. "Years of healing and helping have saturated the space with a positive and uplifting vibration," she says.

Address 133 S State Street, Westerville, OH 43081, +1 (614) 948-5088,
www.mysticnirvana.com | Getting there Bus 43 to S State Street & E Walnut Street |
Hours Wed–Fri noon–7pm, Sat 11am–6pm | Tip Believers in holistics and the
Otherverse will find kindred spirits at the Universal Life Expo, an annual gathering of
psychics, mediums, and the latest in 'new thought' and alternative medicine (Ohio Expo
Center & State Fair, 717 E 17th Avenue, Columbus, OH 43211, www.10times.com/ule).

72__National Barber Museum

Much ado about mutton chops

Like barbering itself, the oldest legal profession in the world, this hirsute hoard has endured. Established in 1988, by Ed Jeffers, the 'Godfather of Barbering,' the museum was originally located in a building that Jeffers owned and lived in. In his five decades as a haircutter, Jeffers also owned and ran several barbershops, along with serving on state/national boards and being written about in textbooks. His collection, which began as a few items of memorabilia, expanded faster than naturally curly hair on a humid Ohio day.

Jeffers' 2006 death left the museum's future at split ends and a 2014 fire forced its relocation. The drive to acquire the museum was spearheaded by current curator/director Mike Ippoliti who persuaded the Canal Winchester Historical Society to take ownership. Space was tight when the fire hit; most of the artifacts were saved, although many had extensive smoke damage. Contributions keep on coming to the new site, which reopened in May 2018.

Now located in a former junior high school, the much larger, six-room museum is a barbering history blowout. Offerings include over 2,000 shaving mugs, a rare collection of now-illegal badger hair shaving brushes and 19th-century barber chairs, like Civil War, pre-hydraulic numbers, and a child's featuring a carved horse head (cue *Godfather* theme). Barber stations of different eras share space with over 70 colorful poles, whose gory roots harken back to the practice of bloodletting. Until the 1800s, barbers provided both dental services and surgery, as illustrated by a scary-looking 16-lancet spring-loaded device.

Among the other odd styling tools are an octopus-like 1920s perm machine and a Faradic Vibrator, which sounds more suited to another ancient profession. The National Barber Hall of Fame includes Vernon Winfrey, who still cuts hair in Nashville. You may have heard of his daughter.

Address 135 Franklin Street, Canal Winchester, OH 43110, +1 (614) 833-1846, www.nationalbarbermuseum.org, mike@nationalbarbermuseum.org | **Getting there** By car, take I-70 E or I-270 S to 33E N High Street in Canal Winchester, then take Washington Street to Franklin Street | **Hours** By appointment only | **Tip** Eat like a local at the Canal Wigwam Restaurant, which was located at the original site of the museum, and tour the still-quaint but refurbished downtown (4 S High Street, Canal Winchester, OH 43110, www.canalwigwam.com).

73 National Veterans Memorial and Museum

Honoring veterans, not war

Replacing the old Veterans Memorial, which offered some services to vets and was the site of concerts, gem shows, and more, is the National Veterans Memorial and Museum (NVMM), a sleek, spiral spaceship of a building, one of *Architectural Digest*'s most anticipated structures of 2018. Within more than 50,000 square feet, the experience starts at the spacious Great Hall overlooking the Scioto River. Rotating exhibits, such as the 'then and now' portraits by combat photographer Stacy Pearsall, provide the first inkling that this is not your grandpa's tribute to military history.

"We wanted to tell the personal stories of the veterans – the decision to serve, the actual service itself, and coming home or being among the fallen – rather than focus on battles and monuments," explains tour guide Kathy Simcox as she and a visitor follow the circular concrete road to the main exhibition galleries.

The museum's uncluttered, almost sparse décor is brought into relief by a timeline of US military history starting with the Revolutionary War. Across the hall are alcoves focusing on various conflicts that offer up slices of individual lives, marrying traditional memorabilia such as letters, photos, and personal effects, with 21st-century touchscreens and video clips.

Open up a replica of war trunks or their like and listen to recording of vets and their civilian families. Other galleries illustrate community contributions and themes of service. Visitors can add information about a veteran to a national database. A 2.5-acre memorial grove, with elm trees, cascading water, and a reflecting pool, rounds out the experience.

"Our goal is not to enlist, but rather to educate as to what it means to serve and offer your life up for your country," adds Simcox.

Address 300 W Broad Street, Columbus, OH 43215, +1 (888) 987-6866, www.nationalvmm.org | Getting there Bus 10 or 12 to W Broad Street & Belle Street | Hours Wed–Sun 10am–5pm | Tip Also heartfelt is the Gahanna Veteran's Memorial, a small plaza with granite benches and a time capsule made from materials taken from the original Veteran's Memorial as well as engraved bricks honoring local vets (73 W Johnstown Road, Gahanna, OH 43230, www.gahannavets.org).

74__Newark Earthworks

When worlds collide over land and over time

Built by the ancient Hopewells with a sophistication far ahead of their time, the Newark Earthworks is aligned with the solstices and was used as a calendar. It also served as burial and ceremonial grounds for the Native people. This 2,000-year-old earthworks, the largest remaining set of geometric enclosures in the world, along with Ohio's Hopewell Culture National Historical Park and Fort Ancient State Memorial, has been nominated as a UNESCO World Heritage Site, of which there are only 23 in the US.

The four-square-mile Newark site consists of monumental geometric enclosures interconnected by a series of low walls. While much of it was destroyed by the settlers, three major sections survived. The Octagon Earthwork has eight walls, each measuring 5 to 6 feet tall and 550 feet long, enclosing an area of 50 acres, and it is also the site of sacred prayer mounds. The Great Circle Earthworks, nearly 1,200 feet in diameter with 8-foot walls surrounded by a 5-foot moat, has a dramatic opening to accommodate large numbers of tribespeople. The Wright Earthworks is a relatively undamaged segment of the original complex.

There is, however, an issue involving the Moundbuilders Country Club, which is built on the Octagon Mound. In 1910, the Ohio History Connection (OHC), in need of funding, leased the land to the country club owners, who built a clubhouse and an 18-hole golf course on the land. The lease was renewed again in 1997 and was supposed to extend until 2078. But the golf course must be removed in order for the World Heritage Site nomination to go forward. The OHC has been in negotiations with the country club, but the parties could not agree on terms. So the case is now being decided in court. Regardless of the outcome, future generations will understand the significance of this site to local history and to the history of the world.

Address 455 Hebron Road, Heath, OH 43056, +1 (740) 344-0498, www.ohiohistory.org/
visit/museum-and-site-locator/newark-earthworks | Getting there By car, take OH-161 E
to OH-37 E to OH-16 E to OH-79 S, exit toward Heath/Hebron Road | Hours Fri–Sun,
noon–4pm, other hours by appointment | Tip Also managed by the OHC, the nearby
Great Circle Museum explains the significance of the Earthworks to Native American
Culture along with how the structures align with the rising and setting of the moon
(455 Hebron Road, Heath, OH 43056, www.ohiohistory.org).

75__Newport Music Hall
Grand dame of rock 'n' roll

You might walk right by the Newport Music Hall in the bustling area around OSU… until the music starts. Generations of students and others have fond memories of rocking out to everyone from Pearl Jam to Anthrax and many more greats and not-so-greats.

Oddly, this grungy, somewhat cramped venue is a favorite of the artists themselves, even though beer is spilled on stage, the wiring can be tricky, and headbanging and crowdsurfing are up close and personal. The lack of regulations, noise and otherwise, appealed to musicians such as Ted Nugent, who reputedly played one of the loudest shows ever heard. Gene Simmons of Kiss handed out candles when the power went out during a thunderstorm. And Joe Walsh of the Eagles said in a 2008 documentary about the venue, "There's no such thing as a bad gig here." Hopefully that's true for blues guitarist and singer John Lee Hooker, who performed his last show ever at the Newport shortly before his 2001 death.

"America's Oldest Continually Running Rock Club," which outlasted the legendary Whiskey a Go Go and Filmore West, among others, began life in 1923 as a movie theater. Rebranded as the Agora Ballroom in 1970, it was purchased by the entertainment booking powerhouse PromoWest in 1984, updated and repaired, and then reopened as the Newport Music Hall, with none other than Neil Young as the first headliner.

The plain brown wrapper of an outside is fairly well preserved, as is the ballroom-like interior. There's nothing refined, however, when it's filled to its 1,700-person capacity, a first floor and balcony crammed with screaming fans. A wide-ranging roster of performances draws a stampede of an annual estimated 150,000 guests.

"It's a jewel," former Columbus radio personality Daddy Wags said in the documentary. "It's maybe not the most polished of jewels, but it definitely has retained its value."

Address 1722 N High Street, Columbus, OH 43201, +1 (614) 294-1659, www.newportmusichall.org | Getting there Bus 2 to N High Street & E 13th Avenue | Hours See website for schedule | Tip OSU's modern, relatively new Ohio Union across the street offers a large and elegant port for students and others to eat and hang out before the show (1739 N High Street, Columbus, OH 43210, www.ohiounion.osu.edu).

76__Ode to Arnold
Schwarzenegger is back to stay

In 1970, an ambitious, young, Austrian bodybuilder named Arnold Schwarzenegger came to Columbus to compete for the Mr. World title. Against all odds, he beat out Sergio Oliva, the incumbent champion. While in Columbus, he also made the acquaintance of the event's organizer, businessman and former FBI agent Jim Lorimer. "Arnold said, 'This is best event I've ever been to and, when I'm done competing … I'm going to come back to Columbus and ask you to be my partner'," stated Lorimer in a 2019 interview. After becoming a five-time Mr. Universe and seven-time Mr. Olympia winner and making a couple of movies you might have heard of, the Terminator himself teamed with Lorimer to create the Arnold Classic in 1989. Today, in front of the Convention Center, is a permanent homage to Arnold in full muscular, sinewy, gun-flexing glory in the form of an 8-foot, 600-pound, scantily clad, bronze statue. And just in case you don't recognize him, the word *Arnold* is emblazoned on the base.

Originally held at Veteran's Memorial with a focus on bodybuilding and, for a heftier fee, a chance to shake hands with the man himself, what became the Arnold Sports Festival over the years exploded, Terminator-like, into the world's largest multi-sport festival, taking over the huge Columbus Convention Center and other venues and bringing millions of dollars and invaluable exposure to the city.

The statue has an outsized provenance as well, and, in fact, an identical one exists in the Schwarzenegger Museum in his hometown of Graz, Austria. Created by sculptor Ralph Crawford, who also made smaller statues to give out as prizes to bodybuilders, the Columbus statue was initially installed outside the old Veteran's Memorial in 2012. Two years later it was relocated and rededicated, where practically every visitor to the city can have their picture taken with the ex-Governator at no extra cost.

Address 486 N High Street, #474, Columbus, OH 43215, www.arnoldsportsfestival.com | **Getting there** Bus 13, 72, 74, CBUS, or SmartBlue to Vine Street & N Park Street | **Hours** Unrestricted | **Tip** Each March at the Arnold Sports Festival, more than 22,000 athletes compete in over 80 sports and events ranging from dance and fitness to boxing to table tennis to axe throwing to swimming, with 600+ vendors and tens of thousands of fitness enthusiasts (400 N High Street, Columbus, OH 43215, www.arnoldsportsfestival.com).

77 Ohio Penitentiary

From grim to glitz

When you go partying in the Arena District, remember that you may be walking on the very ground where the notorious Ohio Penitentiary once stood, at one point housing over 5,200 prisoners in a space intended for 2,000. In August 1995, then-Mayor 'Buck' Rinehart authorized the use of a wrecking ball on the deserted building, without consulting historians or preservationists or getting a permit or study required when demolishing historic structures.

While the resulting outcry from this lack of impulse control failed to stop the eventual razing, it did raise awareness of its fascinating backstory. Built in 1834, the forbidding, two-acre fortress saw both villains and some future heroes. At various times, it hosted Confederate General John H. Morgan, gangster 'Bugs' Moran, and Dr. Sam 'The Fugitive' Sheppard, as well as O. Henry and Chester Himes, who eventually became famous writers.

Along with numerous riots and two major fires – an April 1930 conflagration that killed 322 inmates is considered one of the worst in prison history – it served as a test lab for the development of Old Sparky, the electric chair. Some 315 men and women were put to death in the chair, and their deaths were not always immediate or humane, although some might call the method an improvement over public hangings.

Nonetheless, some strides were made toward creating better conditions. For example, an exercise yard and cells replaced straw mats and open torture. But life in the Pen remained brutal and uncomfortable. Due in part to a 1968 riot and the public's demand for more humane treatment of prisoners in the 1970s, inmates were transferred to other, supposedly more enlightened institutions. The Ohio Penitentiary closed in 1979 and became abandoned.

All that remain are souvenir bricks coveted by collectors and the raucous, crowds around Nationwide Arena.

Address Bounded by Spring Street, Neil Avenue, West Street, & Maple Street, Columbus, OH 43215 | Getting there Bus 1 to N High & Nationwide Boulevard; bus 5, 6, or 9 to W Nationwide Boulevard & N Front Street | Hours Unrestricted | Tip Score your own ice time at OhioHealth Ice Haus in Nationwide Arena, where the Blue Jackets hockey team practices too (200 W Nationwide Boulevard, Columbus, OH 43215, www.arenadistrict.com/listing/ohiohealth-ice-haus).

78__Ohio School of Falconry
Bird's the word

While the thought of walking around with a Harris or red-tailed hawk seems cool in a *Game of Thrones* sort of way, in order to gain the bird's cooperation, you may find parts of a dead chick on your highly gloved arm. As with many animals, these birds of prey are motivated by "trust and snacks," owner and master falconer Joe Dorrian told *Columbus Monthly*, the key word here being "prey." If you can get past a bit of raw meat, then it's all good.

Opened in 2014, the Ohio School of Falconry (OSF), the only one of its kind in the state, was an instant sensation, topping Internet 'must do' lists and attracting school and corporate groups. Its varied programs include weekend Walks with Hawks and Introduction to Falconry events during the clement months, in which Dorrian and his staff teach participants about the sport of falconry and the birds themselves, and participants get the rare chance to interact with them. An occasional Owl Encounter explains more about those particular raptors and their role in falconry, along with photo opportunities with the birds. Sounds like a hoot.

Although falconry has been around for some 4,000 years, requirements for becoming a falconer are rigid and demanding. According to OSF, falconers must complete a two-year apprenticeship and pass a long and difficult written exam, and they must also trap, house, and train a juvenile bird.

Care and accommodations for the birds are also highly regulated. Dorrian, whose lifelong love of falconry began at age 12, also has a day job and a family, along with over 15 years' experience working with the birds.

Once you meet Sedosa, a female Harris's hawk, Chase, an eastern red-tailed hawk, falcons Shelly and Faith, owls Hensen and Dr. Hoo, and the rest of the flock, you will probably become enraptured by your contact with these birds. Just be mindful of their powerful talons.

Address 7925 N High Street, Columbus, OH 43235, +1 (614) 312-5004, www.ohioschooloffalconry.com | Getting there Bus 1 to E Livingston Avenue & Chelsea Avenue, about a 1-minute walk | Hours By appointment only | Tip The Ohio Wildlife Center offers educational programming for all ages including camps, on-site and outreach programs and workshops, and you can volunteer for anything from animal care to answering their rescue hotline (6131 Cook Road, Powell, OH 43065, www.ohiowildlifecenter.org).

79__Old Governor's Mansion
Governing the ghost

High atop Columbus' 'most haunted' lists is the Old Ohio Governor's Mansion – not to be confused with the current Ohio Governor's residence (see ch. 41). Originally built in 1904 by businessman Charles Lindenberg (not to be confused with aviator Charles Lindbergh), the original digs were purchased by the state in 1919. So why, after less than four decades, would the residence be ditched in 1957 for a not-that-much-newer model?

The official explanation was that the 'old' mansion, which the state originally renovated at great cost, was so dilapidated that the 1957 offer of a donation of a replacement was eagerly accepted, even though it too needed significant work. Yet one wonders if other, more supernatural influences were at work here. The first mansion was supposedly inhabited by the ghost of a Lindenberg servant, a Black woman in a blue dress who, according to HauntedHouses.com, "had an unfortunate accident where she may have suffered burns and died from them." Along with glimpses of the apparition, there have also been reports of "the unmistakable odor of burning hair/and probably flesh." That would not have been conducive to hosting parties and gatherings of dignitaries.

Yet the ornate, Georgian-style home had its champions. Originally constructed by famous architect Frank Packard, it boasted nine bedrooms, a ballroom, Tiffany stained-glass windows and lots of gorgeous wood. So after being rescued by the local preservationist Columbus Landmarks Foundation, it was purchased in the late 1990s by the nonprofit Columbus Foundation, who undertook further restoration, although the adjacent Firestone Mansion, also included in the deal, ended up having to be razed, much to the dismay of local history buffs.

Still, someone else was pleased. The ghost supposedly appeared before a worker at the original mansion, expressing delight with the upgrade.

Address 1234 E Broad Street, Columbus, OH 43209, +1 (614) 251-4000, www.columbusfoundation.org, contactus@columbusfoundation.org | **Getting there** Bus 10 to E Broad Street & S Champion Avenue, or 22 to Governor Place & E Broad Street | **Hours** By appointment only | **Tip** Another architectural curiosity is the Flatiron Building, a four-story, wedge-shaped construction built circa 1915 (129 E Nationwide Boulevard, Columbus, OH 43215).

80__Orton Geological Museum

Tell Jeff we said hello

On display in Orton Hall, the oldest building on OSU's campus, amid fossils, minerals and bones, some dating back millions of years, is the skeleton of a large theropod. *Cryolophosaurus ellioti* was found in Antarctica in 1990 by its namesake, Professor David Elliot. In 2018, a replica was mounted in the lobby of Orton Hall. The beast stands, large and in charge, waiting to snack on visitors. The original fossil is in the Field Museum in Chicago.

The museum's other bony superstars, also mostly reproductions, are more locally based. *Megalonyx jeffersonii,* found in Ohio and affectionately known as Jeff, is a seven-foot-tall giant ground sloth named after Thomas Jefferson. Some of the original bones do remain, and they are usually lighter in color. *Dunkelosteus,* a 20-foot-long carnivorous fish, lived in the state when it was covered by a tropical ocean 380 million years ago. The provenance of the *Tyrannosaurus rex* skull and giant South American armadillo are a bit murkier.

Curator Dale Gnidovec has been at the museum for over 30 years. He is full of humorous and fascinating anecdotes, bringing to life the smaller exhibits that also comprise this one-room show, with glass cases, typewritten descriptions and push-button technology that recall museums of the mid-20th century. Although a black-light display of beautiful fluorescent minerals is about as glitzy as it gets, you can spend hours examining relics from Ohio's various geological periods, beginning with the Precambrian era, some 600 million years prior, and dating back to the formation of the Earth. Ohio-based minerals, meteorite shards, and mastodon teeth are other highlights.

Gnidovec speaks to school groups and does extensive community outreach to keep up enthusiasm about these old bones. "Kids love dinosaurs and that's what gets them hooked on science."

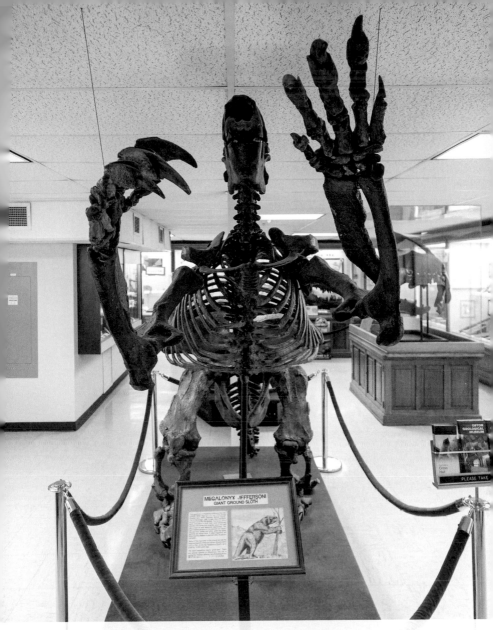

Address 155 S Oval Mall, Columbus, OH 43210, +1 (614) 292-6896, www.ortongeologicalmuseum.osu.edu | Getting there Bus 8, 22, or 31 to 153 W 12th Avenue–Hale Hall, cross the South Oval, or SmartBlue bus to OSU Oval | Hours Mon–Fri 8am–4pm | Tip With a turret-like tower hosting 12 bells, a tower clock, and 24 prehistoric 'grotesques,' Orton Hall, named after Edward Orton Sr., OSU's first president (1878–1881), boasts a library as well as abundant historical, architectural, and geological oddities (155 S Oval Mall, Columbus, OH 43210).

81__Otherworld

A mad science immersive art experience

Visitors to the 32,000-square-foot Otherworld are plunged into a long hallway ending in mirrors with rooms full of kitschy and creepy weird science on either side. Where do you even start? That may depend on whether you are with a small child or fellow geeks. Either way, it is helpful to know the premise of the experience. The story for the experience here is that you are a product tester for a company experimenting in "alternate realm tourism" left on your own to "discover a gateway to bioluminescent dreamscapes featuring alien flora, primordial creatures and expanses of abstract light and geometry," per their website.

For kids, that would be spaces full of fuzzy monsters, beds, and furniture; walls where you can 'color' pictures with your hand; and cubby holes to crawl through to get from one room to the next, including a ginormous, whale-shaped creature which serves as an impromptu hidden playground (adults can enter at their own risk). There is a retro arcade room where you can zap favorite – now vintage – video game characters, triggering a light show. You can and are encouraged to touch everything. (Pro tip: germaphobes might want to bring hand sanitizer.)

Other areas, such as a black-light room crammed with various sizes of animatronic spiders and webs and a Church Room with ominous clowns and coffins you can open, are more suitable for teenagers and older. The experience ends in the Infinity Hallway, where mirrors and flashing LED light poles provide an endless funhouse of exploration.

The brainchild of twenty-something founder and creative director Jordan Renda and some 40 local artists, Otherworld, which opened in 2019, is an exciting and creative experiment that combines creativity, science, and fun into an experience that sends all your senses into overload. So pay attention because you don't want to miss any of it.

Address 5819 Chantry Drive, Columbus, OH 43232, +1 (614) 868-3631, www.otherworldohio.com | **Getting there** Take bus 25 to Chantry Drive at 2nd Service Road Entrance | **Hours** Thu & Sun 11am–8pm, Fri & Sat 11am–10pm | **Tip** The truly adventuresome and their friends, families, and coworkers will enjoy a trip to Breakout Games, which offers a variety of themed breakout rooms, like a kidnapping, an island escape, a mystery mansion, and more (835 Grandview Avenue, Columbus, OH 43215, www.breakoutgames.com/columbus).

82—Palace Theatre

Fabulous workhorse

Built in 1926 as a combo movie and vaudeville theater and designed after France's Palais de Versailles, the Palace Theatre is rich with history, both onstage and off. It has managed to prevail against great odds, such as in the 1970s, when the late Katherine LeVeque rescued the crumbling venue from the wrecking ball. Along with taking away a few seats to allow for more legroom and larger rear ends, a recent renovation added sparkle to the marble floors and chandeliers, repaired plaster carvings, and replaced wall coverings.

This longevity is due in part to excellent acoustics, originally designed so vaudeville performers could be heard without amplification, and continued maintenance of non-cosmetic improvements. "People don't care about the heater until it doesn't work or the roof until it leaks," the theater's Todd Bemis told *Columbus Monthly*.

Also behind the scenes is a performer-friendly downstairs area. Similar to a hotel, it had a 'front desk' where artists could pick up keys and mail, a kitchen, and a playroom for children. A special backstage bath for animal acts, as well as a ramp for easy entry/exit were other extras, along with drawings depicting entertainers – and they were legion. A-list vaudevillians and first-run 'talkie' stars and, during the Depression and WWII, live acts, such as Mae West and big bands like Tommy Dorsey performed here. In fact, you might be hard-pressed to find a performer who has not graced its stage.

In 1989, LeVeque essentially gave the Palace to the Columbus Association for the Performing Arts (CAPA) group of theaters with a renewable, 99-year lease. As home to CAPA-presented and touring troupes, Broadway in Columbus, and local arts organizations, this 2,691-seat workhorse rarely sees a dark night.

Should you have the good fortune to get backstage, you might find that what goes on back there to be as interesting as what's happening onstage.

Address 34 W Broad Street, Columbus, OH 43215, +1 (614) 469-9850, www.capa.com/venues/detail/palace-theatre | **Getting there** Take buses 7, 9, 52, or 61 to N High & W Broad Streets | **Hours** See website for schedule | **Tip** Slightly larger and equally if not more ornate, the gilded, baroque-style Ohio Theatre boasts a 21-foot-high chandelier and an equally impressive roster, including the ever-popular, seasonal *Nutcracker Ballet* (39 E State Street, Columbus, OH 43215, www.capa.com).

83 __ The Palm House
People in glass houses

Today, the Palm House at the Franklin Park Conservatory is where you can take Zumba and gourmet cooking classes, among others, and stop by the annual Hat Day fundraiser, where tickets go for $350 a pop. It stands approximately where General William T. Sherman gave his famous 1880 speech, "War is Hell." In the 1920s, it was also home to the original inhabitants of the Columbus Zoo.

Built in 1895 and modeled after the Glass Palace at the World's Columbian Exposition in Chicago, what is now officially known as the John F. Wolfe Palm House is one of five remaining Victorian glass houses in the US. The referenced palms in question are some of the around 40 tree species as well as an original planting of a fiddle-leaf fig tree.

But the real star in the conservatory's oft refurbished centerpiece is the spectacular double grand staircase that descends into the tropical palm garden, with its gazebos and Venetian fountain, and the lofty glass roof, which lets in plenty of natural light for the plants inside. Another highlight is a sundown-to-sunup computer display with approximately 7,000 LED lights that blankets the structure. Created by artist James Turrell in 2008, the first of its kind in the US, it transitions through a rainbow of color and is best viewed from outside the conservatory.

In 2004, the conservatory acquired a $7-million collection from glass artist Dale Chihuly. Vivid and often oversized, these striking and colorful pieces can be found throughout, complemented by temporary exhibits by other artists in various media.

The conservatory is also home to over 400 plant species found in biomes that mimic the desert, rainforest, mountains, and Pacific Islands, as well as displays of bonsai, succulents, orchids, and more. The 13-acre grounds include a grand mall, community garden, and theme gardens for children, brides, and ornamental grasses.

Address 1777 E Broad Street, Columbus, OH 43203, +1 (614) 715-8000, www.fpconservatory.org, info@fpconservatory.org | Getting there Bus 10 to E Broad Street & N Nelson Road | Hours Daily 10am–5pm | Tip Franklin Park, the nearly 60-acre green space that surrounds the conservatory, is a destination in its own right, with a pond, playground, picnic area, hiking trails, sculptures and water accents from AmeriFlora, the international horticultural exhibition which drew some 2.2 million visitors to Columbus in 1992 (1755 E Broad Street, Columbus, OH 43203, www.columbus.gov/recreationandparks).

84_Perkins Observatory
Space place

Nothing to do on a Friday night? After purchasing tickets in advance, head up to Perkins Observatory for a star-studded evening…maybe. After an orientation and safety reminders – you'll be around expensive and one-of-a-kind equipment in the dark – you will be treated to a humorous and informative talk on the mysteries of the Universe. Then it's onto the main event with a tour of the observatory and, weather permitting, a viewing of the night sky from the dome's 32-inch telescope, one of the biggest in the state. You may get to peer through smaller telescopes on the lawn, although the encroaching city lights of Columbus and nearby Delaware can contribute to less-than-ideal conditions.

This is a classic observatory, not surprising since Perkins has been around since 1923. It lost its major funding from OSU 50 years later to institutions with bigger and more powerful telescopes. So today it is staffed mostly by volunteers.

But what a history! Funded by Hiram Perkins, a wealthy pig farmer and mathematics and astronomy professor at Ohio Wesleyan University, the original telescope with its 69-inch mirror, the third-largest in the world at that time, wasn't completed until 1931, several years after Hiram had passed away. Astronomers came from all over to view and study, but due to city lights and unpredictable weather, in 1961 the telescope was relocated to Lowell Observatory near Flagstaff, Arizona. But thanks to technological advances that created even larger and more durable mirrors, the original mirror was soon returned to Central Ohio, first on loan to the Center of Science and Industry (COSI), then back to Perkins for display.

Perkins also has other special programs and an adult lecture series. You may also encounter Hiram's ghost, who is apparently irritated because you get to look through the telescope he paid for but never got to use.

Address 3199 Columbus Pike, Delaware, OH 43015, +1 (740) 363-1257, www.perkins.owu.edu | **Getting there** By car, I-270 to 23 N/Columbus Pike | **Hours** See website for public events schedule | **Tip** Smaller but with zippier technology in the form of a state-of-the-art XD digital projection system, the 63-seat, 30-foot dome theater at the Ohio State Planetarium offers amazing views across and deep into the night sky (Smith Laboratory, 174 W 19th Avenue, Columbus, OH 43210, www.planetarium.osu.edu).

85 Phoenix Bats
The Cadillac of baseball bats

Who knew that something seemingly as simple as a wooden bat could be so complex and fascinating? The people at Phoenix Bats know, as do those who take their factory tour.

Even the most sports-impaired people might find themselves intrigued by the display of colorful bats at the entry. You'll also encounter the world's most advanced bat manufacturing machine, a computerized number that turns out bats quickly to precise, custom specifications, almost as if by magic. After that, it's onto the dipping, drying, and finishing process, and, for some bats, engraving, which is done lightly so as to not interfere with structural integrity. Along the way, you'll learn about the pros and cons of the northern white ash vs. rock maple vs. yellow birch bats, the choice of which depends upon hitting speed and placement, power, and experience. At the very end, you'll get the cutest mini-bat ever, and if your pocketbook isn't bowled over by, say, a $20 Alien Extractor, Zombie Whacker, or Clown Thumper model, you may find yourself tempted by the occasionally equally humorous selection of clothes, hats, and other assorted accessories, including gloves, baseballs, and even a deluxe bat travel case.

Yet as an official supplier since 2000 to Major League Baseball teams, Phoenix Bats also equips a vast selection of vintage ball teams, softball, and baseball. Along with the big, minor, and little leagues, their customers include schools, hobbyists, and historians. In fact that's how Phoenix got started, rising from the efforts of house restorer Charles 'Lefty' Trudeau. He played vintage baseball for the Ohio Historical Society Muffins in the mid-1990s and was asked to make authentic 1860s wooden baseball bats. Word and sales spread quickly, and Phoenix Bats moved from a small wood shop to their current digs in Plain City, attracting employees, players, and tourists along the way.

Address 7801 Corporate Boulevard, Suite E, Plain City, OH 43064, +1 (614) 873-7776, www.phoenixbats.com | Getting there By car, take I-270 N to OH-161 W/Post Road in Dublin to exit 106, W/US-33 W, then OH-161 W, Industrial Parkway/Old US Highway 33 and Corporate Boulevard | Hours Call for tour information | Tip Popcorn production (and eating), another all-American pastime, can be found at Al's Delicious Popcorn, which also offers tours and tastings of its over 60 varieties (1500 Bethel Road, Columbus, OH 43220, www.alspopcorn.com).

86 _ Pins Mechanical Company

Back to the future

Pins Mechanical Company, a game bar housed in the former National Tire and Battery store, boasts the world's largest ping-pong paddle, some 11.5 feet long. The linchpins – or perhaps more accurately, duckpin bowling and pinball – for the burgeoning Pins franchise also include ping-pong, easily located thanks to the Texas-sized paddle, along with foosball. Not only does each game have a league and/or group of core players of its own, but fierce rivalries can be fueled by an impressive list of craft libations, including brews, cocktails, and punches – the drinking kind. Luckily few if any actual punches are thrown, since the stakes are usually bragging rights only.

While the concept behind such mayhem – and it is often crowded and noisy – may seem casual, the execution is not. Sussing a groundswell based on the earlier success of arcade-based bars and restaurants in Gen X/Y-intensive cities, owner and founder Troy Allen opened this flagship Pins in 2016 to much acclaim, declaring the venues also to be family-friendly before 8pm to attract those with kids in tow and aging Baby Boomers looking for a blast from the past before their pre-Jimmy Kimmel bedtimes. Throw in on-trend repurposing of tire/oil change garage bays into duckpin bowling lanes, a sensory overload lineup of pinball machines ranging from *Black Knight* (1980) to *Iron Maiden* (2018), and a huge, dramatic, greenhouse-style skylight, and it's a turkey – three bowling-type strikes in a row. Other retro touches include classic, oversized board games, as well as a cluster of comfy lounges and a generous outdoor patio.

But with minimalist wood accents, industrial finishes, a party tower, and other spaces available for private gatherings and raucous sports events (think Blue Jackets hockey), this place is a playground for the 21st century.

Address 141 N 4th Street, Columbus, OH 43215, +1 (614) 464-2255, www.pinsbar.com/columbus | Getting there Bus No. 7, 11, 41, 42, 43, 44, 45, or 46 to E Long Street & N 4th Street | Hours Mon–Wed 4pm–1am, Thu & Fri 4pm–2:30am, Sat noon–2:30am, Sun noon–1am | Tip Serious old-school gamers might want to visit Pin's older, smaller sister, the 16-Bit Bar + Arcade a few blocks away. Along with libations named after '80s icons such as Cyndi Lauper and David Hasselhoff, you can play *Donkey Kong*, *Frogger*, and the like and fight for a place on the leaderboard (254 S 4th Street, Columbus, OH 43215, www.16-bitbar.com/columbus).

87 Port Columbus Airport

Homegrown aviation history

"At 7:35 a.m. on July 8, 1929, thousands of spectators watch as passengers arrive at the Columbus railroad station across from the Fifth Avenue, Port Columbus terminal…By 8:17 a.m. 19 passengers, including famed aviatrix Amelia Earhart, are airborne aboard two Ford Tri-Motor aircraft destined for Oklahoma," states the Columbus Airports website.

Thus begins the long and storied history of what was originally known as Port Columbus – so named to make it stand out from the crowd of nascent city airports. Not that it didn't already. Aviator Charles Lindbergh chose the site and according to the Columbus Historical Society, it was the eastern origin for the first transcontinental air/rail route and home of America's first commercial airline TAT, later TWA. Back then, passengers arrived in Columbus via train from New York, flew to Oklahoma, and then boarded another train to Los Angeles, all in the then-astounding time of 48 hours on a one-way ticket costing $351.94 in 1929, or the equivalent of $5,280 today. Flight times have certainly come down since then, as has the price of a ticket, fortunately.

By the early 1950s, the city had outgrown the original tower and moved the airport to its current location nearby. The original building was used for offices and then fell into disrepair, despite its elegant art deco brick exterior and historical significance. The 2014 creation of the Columbus Airport Stabilization Fund resulted in challenge grants, and local businesspeople and foundations rallied toward turning it into a museum honoring Ohio aviators hopefully in the future.

With Ohio aviation giants from Orville and Wilbur Wright, aviator Eddie Rickenbacker, and Jerrie Mock, the first woman to fly solo around the world, as well as astronaut John Glenn, after whom the new Columbus Airport was renamed in 2016, there would be no shortage of honorees.

Address 4920 E Fifth Avenue, Columbus, OH 43219 | Getting there Bus 7 to 4569 or 4800 E 5th Avenue | Hours Unrestricted from the outside only | Tip With a new executive terminal and aviation learning center, OSU airport boasts flight school classrooms and simulators, a terminal, meeting rooms, and an observation deck – all in school colors of scarlet and gray of course (2160 W Case Road, Columbus, OH 43017, www.osuairport.org).

88__The Red Stable

Cuckoo Clocks and More

The Red Stable is a microcosm of just about every knickknack ever made. Handmade jewelry, ornaments, candles, bath and body items, stationery, accessories, plants and outdoor garden art, Ohio State memorabilia, local souvenirs, pet toys, seasonal décor, and more are crammed into a mere 1,000 square feet. And that's just the first floor!

The second floor features paintings, prints, and other media by over 100 local artists. Also available are rare and valuable items including vintage German nutcrackers and smokers, as well as hand-carved Black Forest cuckoo clocks. While nutcrackers primarily represented military, religious, and historical figures, smokers depicted everyday individuals in the act of what is now banned in public places. The clocks, produced by the Hekas company in Schonach, Germany, are carved using techniques and styles passed down since 1938 when the company was established by patriarch Helmut Kammerer, despite the trying times ahead.

Constructed in 1872, the original 'little red barn' was at first a horse livery and later a wagon repair shop, eventually servicing automobiles. When what is now German Village fell out of favor after WWI and II, many of the original immigrants fled to other parts of the city, leaving the area to fall into general disrepair. In 1958, a few remaining residents rose up to preserve what hadn't already been destroyed by a wrecking ball and the addition of a highway. German Village was reborn, nurtured by local businesses, and Red Stable emerged in that small barn, the brainchild of successful artist and owner Phil Keintz, as a studio and gift shop featuring Ohio crafts.

The current owners, Jeff Smith and Stevo Roksandic, have expanded its scope, not only physically but online and in social media. But the close-knit community and friendly staff are timeless, and casual browsers are free to roam.

Address 223 E Kossuth Street, Columbus, OH 43206, +1 (614) 867-5300,
www.theredstable.com, info@theredstable.com | Getting there Bus 5 to E Whittier Street
& S 5th Street | Hours Mon–Sat noon–8pm, Sun noon–7pm | Tip Go next door to
indulge your taste buds at the world-famous Schmidt's Sausage House, which features
sausage platters, schnitzel, sauerbraten, cream puffs, and oompah music (240 E Kossuth
Street, Columbus, OH 43206, www.schmidthaus.com).

89 __ Rhodes Tower Observatory
Government building with a view

Atop the 40th floor of the tallest building in Columbus is a non-partisan surprise – an observation deck with the best and cheapest (free) view in town. Bonus: it also boasts the highest bathroom in the city, which also knows no politics.

Named after Ohio's longest-serving governor, the James A. Rhodes Tower houses some 4,000 state employees toiling in 1.2 million square feet of office space. All you'll need is a driver's license or other valid photo identification to get through security. Then it's onto an express elevator and an ear-popping ride up some 629 feet, while trying not to think about what particular parts of the building have been renovated in the 50 or so years since its 1974 construction.

With stunning views and helpful descriptive posters identifying buildings and other landmarks, the observatory is far more compelling than most of what goes on in the floors below. To the north are Nationwide Arena, Huntington Park, and on a clear day, the OSU campus. To the south, the Ohio Statehouse, Columbus Commons, and Franklin County Courthouse. The western view offers up the LeVeque Tower, as well as the Center of Science and Industry Museum (COSI), and the National Veterans Memorial and Museum amid glimmers of the winding Scioto River. The eastern-facing window provides glimpses of the iconic *Columbus Dispatch* sign, Columbus State University, and the Columbus Public Library.

The observatory's artwork is being updated as well. In 2017, Columbus artist Mandi Caskey created the first of several ongoing works that will supplant the current 75-piece collection, much of which is outdated and damaged. Her 28-foot mural depicting native plant life and four seasons features Ohio scenes, like buckeye trees, white-tailed deer, and cardinals.

Of course, the views depend on the weather. But at least you'll be inside if it starts to rain.

Address 30 E Broad Street, Columbus, OH 43215 | **Getting there** Bus 3, 6, 8, or 9 to E Broad Street & S 3rd Street | **Hours** Mon–Fri 9am–5pm | **Tip** Stop for cocktails and designer French cuisine at The Keep, located nearby in the historic but recently restored art deco LeVeque Tower, which is also now home to a hotel, condos, and apartments (50 W Broad Street, Columbus, OH 43215, www.thekeepcolumbus.com).

90___Rubino's Pizza
A matter of taste

Generations of Bexley natives have been raised on Rubino's Pizza and are vigilant in maintaining its honor as the best pies ever to slide out of an oven.

Established in 1954, this unassuming joint hasn't changed a whit, down to its three-item menu (pizza, spaghetti, and salads), bare-bones interior (basic booths and tables and a pinball machine that looks like it hasn't been moved since the 1970s), and method of doing business (cash-only, orders taken with a rotary phone, pizzas packaged in an old-fashioned tented paper sleeve). Delivery and online orders are not an option; you must go in and pick it up yourself. Yet in spite of being next door to the also top-rated Bexley Pizza Plus, as well as several other well-known chains, Rubino's is constantly busy. Especially if you live in Bexley, chances are you'll run into someone you know while you're waiting for your order.

The rest of the world, however, has a somewhat divided opinion. Local food writer G. A. Benton describes it as a "symphony in the key of retro," when singing the praises of its hamburger-dill topped pickle pizza (an acquired taste). Most people, however, opt for pepperoni and sausage, usually with extra cheese, because while Rubino's is generous with the toppings, people always want extra cheese, which, combined with their slightly tangy tomato sauce, cracker-thin crust, and a generous dose of oil, tends to be especially messy as the toppings slide off the ends of the itty-bitty cross-cut slices at the end.

When the original owner Ruben Cohen retired, he sold the pizzeria to Frank Marchese and Tommy Culley. Marchese's children operate it today. Pizza is prepared the way it was back then – all toppings are house made, and the pie is baked in ovens that look like bona fide antiques.

There's only one way to find out whether it's your cup of…pepperoni? Go there and try one for yourself.

Address 2643 E Main Street, Columbus, OH 43209, +1 (614) 235-0712 | Getting there Bus 2 to E Main Street & S Roosevelt Avenue | Hours Tue–Fri 11am–10:30pm, Sat 4–11:30pm, Sun 4–10:30pm | Tip In 1929, the first pizza debuted in Columbus at nearby TAT – named after the first airline in Columbus – which does take credit cards and online orders, while maintaining its blast-from-the-past menu and atmosphere (1210 S James Road, Columbus, OH 43227, www.tatitalianrestaurantcolumbus.com).

91 _Rush Creek Village

Usonian utopia

Tucked away in the New England-style village of Worthington is a well-maintained but jarring-looking enclave of about 50 Frank Lloyd Wright-style houses. Originally called Kook Valley by the locals when it was built in the mid-20th century, Rush Creek Village is now the largest collection of its kind and on the National Register of Historic Places. Not only do residents remain here for decades, but they often pass down homes to their children. "Homeowners… tell of extended lives, long-lasting marriages and above-average children, all nurtured by Wright's Usonian principles," states *The New York Times*. Also controversial back then was the village's lack of covenants against race or religion. "The only discrimination we practice here is architectural," an owner assured the *Times*.

A combination of 'US' and 'useful,' Usonian architecture featured open plans and carports, but often utilized flimsy and impractical construction materials. However, most Rush Creek homes were designed by local architect Theodore van Fossen, who although he studied in Wright's New Bauhaus school, adapted the construction to endure rough Ohio weather while keeping the Wright principles of economies of space, built-in features, and windows, melding landscape and design.

Standouts include the single-floor Round House, which boasts a main house connected by a covered walkway to studio/guest house. Located near the entrance, the five-story Tower House is a cube-like behemoth with three bedrooms, a studio, and enough steps to preclude a gym membership.

In the 1940s, Worthington resident and Rush Creek founder Martha Wakefield and her husband Richard went to Wright's home in the Arizona desert to discuss building their own abode. Wright told her to go home and build a house for herself and then for her neighbors, and that's what she did.

Address Located off of E South Street in Worthington, between Granby Street & White Oak Place, +1 (614) 885-1247, www.worthingtonhistory.org/buildings-and-locations/rush-creek-village | **Getting there** Bus 102 to High Street & South Street, about a 0.3-mile walk | **Hours** Unrestricted from the outside only, tours by appointment only | **Tip** Nearby and equally off the beaten path is the Light of Seven Matchsticks, named after a made-up novel in Wes Anderson's Moonrise Kingdom, with Prohibition-era cocktails and a secret menu of small plates (5601 N High Street, Worthington, OH 43085, www. thelightofsevenmatchsticks.com).

92___Self-Driving Shuttle
Short circuit

With a glass roof and resembling a stretch Kia Soul with two front ends, the Self-Driving Shuttle has four seats in the cheerful-looking green and white vehicle that face each other, practically forcing you to make eye contact with your fellow passengers. A 49-inch digital display provides system and route information, a 1.5-mile foray that stops at the Center of Science and Industry, the National Veterans Memorial and Museum, Bicentennial Park, and the Smart Columbus Experience Center every 10 minutes. And while the shuttle can go up to 25 mph, it's usually slower. It's also possible that the ever-present operator will actually do the driving. Rain, snow, a special event, or road construction may deprive you of the actual experience of having the machine pilot itself, but usually it lives up to its name.

With names like Mimi, Myla, and Mukti, an undoubted nod to their creator, May Mobility (and possibly that OSU rival football state 'up North' where the company is located), the six vehicles are equipped with sophisticated sensor and navigational systems that try to plan for every contingency, such as someone crossing the street in front of the vehicle. It happens a lot, according to the friendly driver, "People see the shuttle, stop, and sometimes stare. I get a lot of questions." He also has a fair amount of regular riders.

The shuttles are part of a $40-million Smart City Challenge granted in 2016 to the City of Columbus, making it the first place in the US to integrate technologies such as self-driving cars, remotely connected vehicles, and smart sensors into its public transportation system. Philanthropies and investments added another cool $500 million to bolster the effort even more.

With limited bus service as the only public transportation option, the city is making strides in the right direction – with or without human drivers.

Address 233 S Civic Center Drive, Columbus, OH 43215, +1 (614) 223-2170, www.smartcircuitcbus.com | **Getting there** Bus 3, 6, or 9 to W Main Street & S Ludlow Street | **Hours** Daily 6am–10pm | **Tip** Hop off the shuttle at the Smart Columbus Experience Center, which offers hands-on displays and information about current 'smart' projects and technology. Coolest of all, you can test-drive the latest in electric vehicles (170 S Civic Center Drive, Columbus, OH 43215, www.smart.columbus.gov).

93 — Short North Street Art

Beauty on once crime-filled streets

Initially named the Short North by police to define the crime-ridden area between downtown and the OSU campus, this 14-block strip has gone from shabby to chic since the 1980s. Its nationally recognized arts scene includes a monthly, jam-packed gallery hop, when dozens of galleries offer everything from folk to fine art. The area boasts an acceptance of public art so mainstream that people can vote for their favorite works á la *American Idol*.

Now-iconic artworks include 17 LED-adorned steel arches on High Street. Installed in 2002, they pay homage to Columbus' Victorian-era nickname 'Arch City', when the wooden gaslit versions erected over 100 years ago had become all the rage. Two whimsical wall murals, an upside-down twist on *American Gothic* and a sideways *Mona Lisa*, as well as sculptures, mosaics, and other media are also permanent installations.

But the most hotly contested honor is having a work selected for the Six in the Short North temporary mural series, started in 2012 with works rotating every 2–3 years. Consisting of high-resolution images of original art works, these vinyl offerings are heat-adhered to buildings throughout the district, providing the illusion of permanence. "Selection of artists was initially based on the recommendations of galleries," explains artist, designer, and community activist Adam Brouillette, whose *Blue Within A Sea of Red* was affixed to 895 N High Street in 2017. Today, however, the public curates the final six via popular vote.

Although not everyone was in sync about that decision and, as with many things affecting the district, says Brouillette "There was a lot of back and forth discussion. The temporary art idea is being adopted in other parts of the city, such as 400 West Rich in Franklinton." Time has certainly changed attitudes toward street art since the days when it was considered vandalism.

Address Various locations along N High Street, Columbus, OH 43215, +1 (614) 299-8050, www.shortnorth.org/arts-galleries/public-art | **Getting there** CBUS free downtown circulator to N High Street | **Hours** Unrestricted | **Tip** Explore the Short North with your friends via the Pedal Wagon, which offers 2-hour, 15-passenger, self-propelled 'cruises' to High Street, Summit Street, and other points of interest, including stops at partner establishments for libations (17 E 6th Avenue, Columbus, OH 43201, www.pedalwagon.com/columbus).

94 _ Sirak Collection
Art for scandal's sake at the CMA

Although the Columbus Museum of Art (CMA) is delightful and diverting, the stories behind its collections are equally compelling. Established in 1878, CMA has grown up with the city. It doubled in size in 2015 and increased its profile even more through the 2018 donation of some 40 works of contemporary art by philanthropists Ron and Ann Pizzuti.

In 1991, another wealthy couple, the late Dr. Howard and Babette Sirak, also offered CMA 78 paintings appraised at $80 million. Included were masters such as Degas, Klee, Renoir, Rodin, and Matisse. Howard Sirak said in a *Columbus Dispatch* interview that they wanted to maintain the collection as a whole.

Works from the Sirak Collection are on display at the CMA, and in 2011, the entire collection, which consists of Impressionist and Expressionist art, including five paintings by Claude Monet, was on exhibit for its 20th anniversary celebration.

Apparently, this desire to keep their worldly goods together extended to their kids' money too. A few months after the donation, the Siraks were sued in court by Vicki, the widow of their late son Bill, whom they had declared to be mentally incompetent, along with his brother Robert. At stake were, among other things, approximately $500,000 of Bill's money, which the Siraks apparently misappropriated for various donations, including $262,500 to pay off their debt on a Renoir that was eventually donated to the museum. While the Siraks claimed they had been trying to protect Bill, who had committed suicide, from kidnappers. Undoubtedly Vicki, against whom they filed a countersuit for the alleged murder of their son, saw things differently. The court wasn't buying their story either. The Siraks dropped the murder charges, and they were ordered to repay some $453,288 plus interest to Vicki, an eventual settlement of some $2.6 million, and justice was served for her husband.

Address 480 E Broad Street, Columbus, OH 43215, +1 (614) 629-0306,
www.columbusmuseum.org | Getting there Bus 10 to E Broad Street & S Washington
Avenue | Hours Tue, Wed, & Fri–Sun 10am–5pm, Thu 10am–9pm | Tip Located in a
separate space, the Pizzuti Collection has themed exhibits from the philanthropists' private
stock in a variety of media with an emphasis on worldwide diversity (632 N Park Street,
Columbus, OH 43215, www.pizzuti.columbusmuseum.org).

95 — Skully's Music Diner

Groove, dance, and dine

Despite being located in the parking-impaired Short North, Skully's has been around for some 25 years, or eons in music-business speak. Their secret? Along with pulling in popular and emerging midsize touring acts such as Twenty-One Pilots, The Black Keys, and superstar rapper Kendrick Lamar in genres ranging from indie rock and punk to metal, folk, and more, the varied lineup – such as Ladies 80s, a Thursday night staple recently changed to Mess Around, 2000's Indies Dance Party – has garnered numerous awards: Best DJ Night, Best Mid-Sized Venue, Best Place to Rock and Roll, and Best Place for Hip Hop. In 2015, Travelog.us named it the "The Best Diner in America."

In 1994, Earl 'Skully' Web, a veteran of the local music scene, opened his namesake saloon in South Campus, moving it to its current location seven years later. The 6,000-square-foot venue is laid out like a mullet, fronted by the bar and restaurant area, and the party in the back, a large space with a stage and a balcony. The patio can offer a welcome respite and a breath of fresh air. The reasonably priced menu includes breakfast, pizza, salads, sandwiches, and many other tasty dishes. A local favorite is the signature Skully Burger, an artery-clogging but reliably delicious mess of a burger with cheese and toppings on a brioche bun.

But a night at Skully's can be like a box of chocolates: you never know what you're going to get on any given night, given the diversity of the bands that play here and the people who show up to hear them. The quality of the sound is one of the main attractions, as is the friendly service. There's a service charge for anyone under 21, and the noise level/lyrics may not always be suitable for every ear. But for anyone looking for a vibrant scene, this is the place to go hear a wide range of music and enjoy a cheese-stuffed pretzel or veggie gyro.

Address 1151 N High Street, Columbus, OH 43201, +1 (614) 291-8856, www.skullys.org |
Getting there Bus 1, 2, or 5 to N High Street & W 4th Avenue | Hours Mon–Fri
11–2:30am, Sat noon–2:30am, Sun 1pm–2:30am | Tip Equally fun is the Varsity Club,
which also has a full menu although the entertainment consists of drinking and yelling at
the TV during various Ohio State sporting events (278 W Lane Avenue, Columbus,
OH 43201, www.varsityclubrestaurantcolumbusoh.com).

96 — Social Justice Park
Moral compass in progress

Here in Columbus, you will find the world's first park dedicated to social justice. At around about 18,000 square feet, Washington Gladden Social Justice Park only recently opened in 2018. It's a $3.7-million class act, with a green space consisting of half-concentric circles converging upon a main gathering area and a long wall highlighting local events, individuals, and their contributions, including the current exhibit, a temporary mural honoring seven early Columbus social justice pioneers.

The entrance sculptures and inspirational quotes for its Pathway to Justice walkway are works in progress. The park will recognize other early hometown crusaders in the future, such as the Society of American Indians and various trade unions.

Yet naming the park after Gladden seems like an unlikely decision. According to Ohio History Central, he was consumed with issues such as the "local government's failure to enforce a law requiring saloons to remain closed on Sundays." And while, "he called for equal rights and opportunities for African Americans with white people, …at the same time, he believed that blacks were naturally inferior to whites," and that "immigrants, especially Catholic immigrants, were lazy and prone to alcoholism."

Well, it *was* the late 1880s. And Gladden, along with being a nationally prominent leader of the Progressives, as liberals were called at the time, was a wildly popular pastor at the First Congregational Church. He was also an outspoken advocate for civil, worker's, women's, and voting rights; integration; the needs of the poor and underserved; and religious tolerance. Plus, the church owns the land the park sits on and spearheaded the effort to create it.

But this park, funded by public monies and private donations, is open to all, and all are welcome to contribute, be it ideas, funds, or time as a volunteer.

Address 404 E Broad Street, Columbus, OH 43215, www.socialjusticepark.org, info@socialjusticepark.org | Getting there Bus 10 to E Broad Street & N Washington Avenue | Hours Unrestricted | Tip Another spiritual pillar of the community, ornately decorated with gorgeous stained glass, is the 1920s-era Annunciation Greek Orthodox Cathedral which celebrates its own brand of diversity at the annual Greek Festival (555 N High Street, Columbus, OH 43215, www.greekcathedral.com).

97__South Drive-in Theatre & Flea Market

A very unique two-fer

It's a flea market! And a drive-in movie theater! South Drive-In Theatre is one of only 24 left in the state and the only one in Columbus. In the morning, you can shop for everything from baseball bats and OSU swag to antique furniture and funky purses, eat lunch at the snack bar, and then return that same evening to watch a double feature from inside your own car.

Established in 1950 as a drive-in, one of about 15 or so in the area during the mid-20th-century heyday of these automotive entertainment venues, the South's flea market opened some 20 years later. The owners "were looking for a way to maximum the return on their investment," explains general manager Bryon Teagardner. Opening up over 300 spaces to anyone who had anything legal to sell, used or new, like cars and boats, CDs/DVDs and baby items, and pretty much anything else, not only resulted in a bargain hunter's free-for-all but also a continual surprise for those who live for Saturday yard sales. Those looking to get rid of stuff need only pay a minimal registration fee (and the $25 vendor's license from the State of Ohio), set up shop between two speaker posts, and make sure their merchandise is lawful – no guns, ammo, or items that have 'fallen off the truck,' please). Sellers generally arrive before 5am to set up their displays, and buyers show up no later than 9am.

Drive-in patrons can treat themselves to a double feature of their choice, partaking of the traditional speakers using FM radio frequency from their car or a portable radio, or a smartphone app. The show goes on, rain or shine, although occasional extreme weather, like a tornado, may close down the drive-in. Unlike traditional theaters, you can also bring your lawn chairs to sit outside and bring a picnic too.

Address 3050 S High Street, Columbus, OH 43207, +1 (614) 491-6771, www.southdrive-in.com | **Getting there** By car, take I-70 E to OH-104 S to US-23 S/S High Street about 1.6 miles to destination | **Hours** See website for movie and flea market hours | **Tip** The adventuresome can check out the indoor/outdoor Westland Flea Market with its extensive *quinceañera* finery, jewelry, and accessories, intriguing selection of Hispanic foodstuffs, and appliances and (non-gun) weaponry of dubious provenance (4170 W Broad Street, Columbus, OH 43228, www.westlandfleamarket.com).

98__Spirit of Women Park
Medical center retreat

Located in the middle of the busy Ohio State Wexner Medical Center, the Chlois G. Ingram Spirit of Women Park offers an oasis to relax in, in front of the Donor Fountain, an area surrounded by wildflowers, dine amid a cluster of handicapped-accessible tables, check your email or Facebook status on the park's free Wi-Fi, or simply contemplate to the sound of the water. The 175-foot, crescent-shaped fountain contains 1,515 life stories in the form of etched-glass tiles just below the surface of the reflecting pool. These are donors from the original Chlois G. Ingram Spirit of Women Park, built in 2001 and named for a hospital volunteer whose family also owned White Castle and donated several million dollars to OSU for research.

In 1999, when the project was first initiated, these colorful, ceramic tiles were painted in a variety of sizes and shapes to honor women, both living and deceased, in the donors' lives. People from all walks of life flocked to sessions where they could design their tiles. The result was as unique and varied as the donors themselves. Some tiles had simple drawings, while others featured detailed quotes and lists of names. Artists were as diverse as Sarah Ferguson, Duchess of York, and fifth-grader Isha Dandavante. Other women, such as cancer survivor Harriet Grail, created tiles to represent their own triumphs and challenges.

By the early 2010s, however, a $1.1-billion expansion of the medical center could have swallowed up the tiny park, with its chipped, fading tiles. Instead, the park was restored and expanded, and the tiles photographed and painstakingly digitally traced. The result is a stunning, mostly black-and-white depiction that stands out during the day and especially at night, when the fountain is illuminated. These tiles tell stories and remind you that life is full of challenges to be faced and overcome.

Address 1585 Westpark Street, Columbus, OH 43210, +1 (614) 257-3060, www.wexnermedical.osu.edu | **Getting there** Bus 22 to 9th Avenue & Medical Center Drive | **Hours** Unrestricted | **Tip** Another go-to body of water at OSU, albeit larger and better known, is historic Mirror Lake, also recently restored and the site of many an engagement (Neil Avenue between John Herrick Drive and Neil Drive, Columbus, OH 43210).

99 __ Statehouse Pigeon

Pigeon run in the Statehouse

One can spend hours gawking at the Greek Revival-style Ohio Statehouse. The Grand Rotunda, with its colorful, light-filtering skylight and Escher-like floor. The gilded elegance of the House Chamber, with its elaborately carved pillars and ceiling tiles, and other handcrafted accents. The plaques, statues, and memorials honoring, among other notables, Abraham Lincoln, George Washington Williams, the first African-American legislator, and Ohio's Holocaust survivors and their WWII veteran liberators. The way-ahead-of-its-time 'forced air' heating system installed after the building was designed because architect Nathan B. Kelley discovered that it lacked heating or ventilation. The flat cupola, rather than the usual dome found on many state capitols, which makes it look perpetually unfinished or at least somewhat odd.

This cupola was one of many points of controversy during the 1839–1861 construction, made even more of a mishmash by the fits and starts of completion as funding ran out or was acquired, despite free labor (prisoners) and firing architects who went over budget. But, since the building was an homage to the Greeks who created democracy, the Greek-style cupola remained, although from the inside, it still looks like a dome. And while the center of government hardly seems like a romantic venue, the Statehouse also hosts weddings.

But the most curious aspect is a stuffed bird called Pete the Pigeon. Before the Atrium, which connected the Statehouse with the Senate Building, was built in 1993, legislators had to run like heck between the two buildings to avoid being splattered with poop from the dozens of pigeons that hung out there. Perched high above the Senate side of the Atrium, Pete is kind of hard to see, even though his coloring was altered to brown, which helps him stand out from the grey building. A fitting commentary on politics if there ever was one.

Address 1 E Capitol Street, Columbus, OH 43215, +1 (614) 752-9777, www.ohiostatehouse.org, visitors@ohiostatehouse.org | **Getting there** Bus 2 to S High Street & E State Street | **Hours** See website for public tours | **Tip** With a stunning Carrara marble staircase/hallway, a stained-glass Great Seal of Ohio skylight, and lots of gold leafing, the adjacent digs of Ohio's state senators is hardly pigeon feed (1 E Capitol Street, Columbus, OH 43215, www.ohiosenate.gov).

100__Thompson Memorial Library

Decking the stacks

Sometimes the best things in life really are free. Take libraries, particularly the William Oxley Thompson Memorial Library. Not only does it offer a bird's-eye view of the Oval, the center of Ohio State's 66-some-thousand-student campus, but there's also great people watching within the library itself. Just look up at the stacks from the multi-level atrium. Originally constructed in the 1950s, several floors of dark and gloomy study areas with hidden carrels and shelves of musty books are now completely glassed-in, practically guaranteeing that you're hitting the books rather than on a cute co-ed. Standing right in front of the library is the statue of its namesake, William Oxley Thompson, Ohio State's fifth president (1899–1925).

As with its football team, Ohio State is fiercely loyal to its library, which was built in 1913, funding major renovations in 1951, 1977, and 2009. The latest three-year, $108.7-million effort returned the library to its original light and airy Beaux Arts beauty. The grand reading room was restored with floor-to-ceiling windows and fronted by a stationary replica of the *Winged Victory* statue originally donated by the class of '92 – 1892, that is. The original statue that was donated, hung 15 feet in the air but was removed in the 1950s because of deterioration and the "perceived danger of…maybe a chunk falling on some student's head," a former library director told the OSU *Lantern*.

Although the library had to shuffle part of its extensive collections elsewhere, student usage has increased, thanks to extensive 21st-century wireless computing and multimedia options; double the seating capacity; and a café. Plus, it has won a number of architectural and adaptive reuse awards.

The Athletics Department, which provided the first $9 million for funding, undoubtedly knew a winning effort when it saw one.

Address 1858 Neil Avenue, Columbus, OH 43210, +1 (614) 292-6785, www.library.osu. edu/locations/thompson | **Getting there** Bus 8 to Neil Avenue & W 11th Avenue | **Hours** Daily 7:30am–midnight | **Tip** Students can exercise off study-related and other stress with the nearby Texas-sized Recreation and Physical Activities Center (RPAC) with some 27,500 square feet of fitness, group sports, and aquatic options (337 Annie and John Glenn Avenue, Columbus, OH 43210, www.recsports.osu.edu).

101 Thurber House
Ghost writer

Constructed circa 1875, what is now Thurber House was purportedly haunted by two separate entities well before the humorist James Thurber and his family took up residence there from 1913 until 1917. It was here that Thurber, a student at OSU, encountered the ghost that inspired one of his best-known short stories, unoriginally titled, *The Night the Ghost Got In*. It might have been a male apparition who supposedly committed suicide during the 1880s after discovering his wife in bed with her lover. (The real story is that in 1904, a prominent local jeweler accidentally fatally shot himself in front of his wife and a female friend.) Thurber then went on to international acclaim as an author, *New Yorker* cartoonist, and Tony Award-winning playwright. The second haunting was supposedly seven ghosts who died in an 1868 fire when the site was part of the larger Ohio Lunatic Asylum, with sightings reported throughout the entire block.

Yet Thurber House is primarily recognized as being a lightning rod for literary lions, both well-known and aspiring. Its many programs include evenings with nationally recognized authors, literary picnics, children and adult writing programs, and the prestigious Thurber Prize for American Humor. There are also adult and children's writer-in-residence programs, one month of uninterrupted writing time in the house plus a stipend. Not a bad payday for a couple of potentially spooky encounters.

Earthly visitors can also stop by the house for a tour, which includes access to the formal parlor, living and dining rooms, bedrooms, "and the bathroom Thurber hid in to avoid the ghost running up the backstairs," states the house's website. Also on display are his artwork, memorabilia, and assorted period pieces "where visitors are invited to sit…and experience the museum as if they were the Thurbers' guests." This presumably includes ghosts as well.

Address 77 Jefferson Avenue, Columbus, OH 43215, +1 (614) 464-1032, www.thurberhouse.org, thurberhouse@thurberhouse.org | Getting there Bus 10 to E Broad Street & Jefferson Avenue | Hours Daily 1–4pm | Tip Test-drive your own creative writing efforts every Wednesday at 8pm at the Writers Block Open Mic poetry night at Kafe Kerouac. Writers' Block also offers writing workshops and other literary-minded events (2250 N High Street, Columbus, OH 43201, www.writersblockpoetry.com).

102__The Top

Rat Pack retro dining

When The Top opened in 1955, $5 bought you a shrimp cocktail appetizer, a ribeye, an oversized baked potato and salad, and one stiff drink. Today, the prices are about the only thing that has changed in this Bexley institution.

This supper club seems excavated from a *Mad Men* set. A copper-embossed piano bar is lined with retirement-age, prosperous-looking regulars anticipating the night's entertainment, most often house pianist and resident matchmaker Sonia Modes, who has been there for decades and even has a parking spot reserved for her Cadillac. The dim, wood-paneled dining room is crammed with leather booths and tables, which are usually packed, even on weeknights. Even the white china plates and oversized menu look pretty much the same as before. Throughout its 60-some years, the restaurant's food has consistently won raves, falling firmly into the "expensive but worth it" steakhouse category. Considering that each entrée comes with two generous sides, it's kind of a bargain when compared to say, Morton's.

Yet The Top, often the favorite gathering spot for local politicians and captains of industry, also has its share of skeletons. A 'whore door' near what was once a private bar that granted only a select few entry with a knock. "They'd say you took your wives to the front bar on Friday and your mistresses to the back bar on Saturday," Regina Adkins, who currently co-owns it with husband and chef Denver Adkins, told *Columbus Monthly*. People also try to steal anything with the Top logo on it, from the plates to wine glasses to a picture of the original Rat Pack in the men's room. The Top also saw a number of celebrities back in the day: Bob Hope, Red Skelton, and the singer Charo, to name a few.

Past patrons may be gone or forgotten, but this top keeps on spinning out charbroiled steaks, jumbo lobster tails, and olive-stuffed vodka martinis.

Address 2891 E Main Street, Columbus, OH 43209, +1 (614) 231-8238, www.thetopsteakhouse.com | Getting there Bus 2 to E Main Street & Enfield Road | Hours Mon–Thu 5–10pm, Fri & Sat 5–11pm | Tip Those looking for a good cut of meat without all the fanfare will find it at the Zagat-rated Hyde Park Steakhouse, a regional chain that got its start in Cleveland (569 North High Street, Columbus, OH 43215, www.hydeparkrestaurants.com).

103__Topiary Park

Panhandler paradise lost

Once the purview of panhandlers in an abandoned space, covered in rubble and debris, that housed the fire-scarred Ohio School for the Deaf, Topiary Park has risen from the ashes to become an attraction that you, or *yew*, to turn a phrase, as yew trees make up its 80-some sculptures, will likely find memorable. A reproduction of Georges Seurat's 1884 painting, *A Sunday Afternoon on the Island of La Grande Jatte*, the arrangement includes fifty-four topiary people, eight boats, three dogs, a monkey, and a cat set around a pond that can almost pass for the River Seine if you stand on the easternmost hill.

Still, there's no denying the charm of a garden full of interesting figures scattered among flowers, sidewalks, and benches. The large green space lends itself to summer concerts and movies, and a cute château-style gatehouse that serves as a visitors' center, although it's not officially open during performances.

But if it weren't for AmeriFlora, a horticultural world's fair that launched in 1992 to mark the quincentennial of Christopher Columbus' arrival in the New World, Topiary Park might never have existed. A few years prior, local sculptor James T. Mason, who worked for the city, and his then-wife Elaine came up with the concept, garnered support from local leaders, and found some generous donors. By the time AmeriFlora opened its doors in April of that year, the park was done, dusted, and dedicated. The City of Columbus boasted the distinct honor of having the world's only green space based entirely on a painting.

The seven-acre park also has bragging rights to around 220 different species of trees. Spending a few hours wandering among trees with names like Princeton Sentry Ginkgo, Bloodgood London Planetree, and Summer Charm Japanese Tree Lilac is a very pleasant way to spend a Saturday afternoon in this island of greenery.

Address 480 E Town Street, Columbus, OH 43215, +1 (614) 645-0197, www.facebook.com/
topiarypark | Getting there Bus 11 to Town & Washington | Hours Daily 7am–11pm | Tip
A short jaunt away is the newly renovated and revitalized Old Towne East neighborhood,
with over 1,000 historic homes and 50 architectural styles, including Italianate, Queen Anne
and Victorian (www.oldetowneeast.org).

104__ Town & Country
The shopping center that refuses to die

Opened in 1949 (or 1956, depending on the source), the Town & Country Shopping Center, one of the world's first open-air, modern shopping malls, is still going strong, even garnering a spot in the Mall Hall of Fame. Yes, there is such a place, although it's virtual, much like retail itself these days.

So what has been the secret of T&C's longevity? For one thing, it's been strategically managed by the privately held Casto company, whose founder, Don M. Casto Sr., started the whole strip mall industry in 1928 with the Grandview Avenue Bank Block, some 30 stores with parking for up to 400 horseless carriages.

Yet when Casto Sr. came up with his post-WWII brainchild in the suburb of Whitehall, remote at the time, deriders referred to it as 'Casto's Folly,' thinking no one would drive that far, say, for a pair of shoes or a set of towels. The subsequent explosion of first the suburban indoor shopping malls (Northland, Southland, Westland) and later, mixed-use retail centers such as Easton Town Center proved them wrong. Casto also kept adding and updating T&C, including opening the first shopping center version of JCPenney, along with Kroger's (eventually closed) and the now-defunct Kresge's 5 & 10 and Union department stores. By the mid-1950s, T&C was also known as the 'Miracle Mile,' although it was actually half that length. But it continued to pack a punch, thanks to two subsequent remodels and updates, one in 1986 and another at the turn of the 21st century, in honor of the 50th anniversary.

While the neighborhood has gone through many changes and developments since those early days, T&C, now located smack in the middle of the suburbs, is still a convenient drive, with offerings ranging from Staples and Shoppers World to Family Dollar and Bob Evans, and, completing the circle of life, a brand-spanking new Kroger Marketplace.

Address 3912 E Broad Street, Columbus, OH 43213, www.castoinfo.com | Getting there Bus 10 to E. Broad Street & Collingwood Avenue about a 1-minute walk | Hours Vary by venue | Tip Along with the usual Chinese menu options, Wings Restaurant, which has also been around in its present location since the 1950s, offers American grub as well as an impressive selection of Scotch (2801 E Main Street, Columbus, OH 43209, www.wingsofbexley.com).

105__Union Station Arch
Doorway to nowhere

Situated in a small park in the middle of the raucous Arena District, this seemingly random, giant terracotta arch is the only remaining part of the bustling and beautiful Union Station that was originally located in the Short North.

Actually, Columbus had three Union Stations. The first was built in 1851 and the second in 1875. The increase in rail and road transportation in a growing city kept causing major traffic jams. By the time No. 3 came around in 1897, even the construction of a pedestrian tunnel couldn't mitigate the problems caused by almost a dozen railroad tracks crossing High Street, not to mention horse-drawn vehicles. Plus the tunnel was narrow, dark and creepy.

So city fathers went all out with the third, hiring famous architect Daniel Burnham and constructing a road viaduct over the tracks. An arcade for stores and businesses was built atop the viaduct, a monumental statement of Beaux Arts Classicism. By 1970, however, the number of daily passenger trains had slowed to a dribble. And while Amtrak took over the station for a few years, it quickly closed, replaced with plans for a new Convention Center and a Hyatt Regency hotel.

The Arcade was listed on the National Register of Historic Places and what is now the Ohio History Connection had plans to save it. But on a Friday night in October 1976, construction crews hit Union Station with a wrecking ball after discussions fell through with the builder about who would pay for its conservation. Fortunately the preservationists had a lawyer who was sympathetic to their cause; he was able to obtain a restraining order from the lone available judge who wasn't attending an OSU home football game. So the arch, the only piece remaining intact, was rescued and later moved to its current location.

A monument to the consequences of miscommunication, it ironically serves as a great landmark for meeting up with friends.

Address W Nationwide Boulevard, Columbus, OH 43215 | Getting there Bus 1 to N High Street & Nationwide Boulevard | Hours Unrestricted | Tip The small, wedge-shaped McFerson Commons Park is host to numerous events and outdoor activities, from a kickball league during the warm months to winter ice skating (218 West Street, Columbus, OH 43215, www.sciotomile.com).

106__Wagner-Hagans Auto Museum

What's in a name?

People who think it's impossible to please everybody should meet Steve Wagner. As chief cook, bottle washer, and curator of what's better known as the Wagner-Hagans Auto Museum, he, or rather his accumulation of mostly mid-20th-century cherry-condition cars, WWI and II vehicles, and odd license plates from around the world, has snagged Columbus' No. 1 spot on TripAdvisor with nary a single negative review (as of this writing). All despite having the exterior trappings of a failed auto-body shop.

But the tour's the thing, along with the robin's egg blue 1956 Chrysler Imperial with push-button drive, the yellow 1957 Nash Ambassador with its spaceship-like hood and front light ornaments, the turquoise 1960 Edsel Ranger with back fins, and the white 1956 Lincoln Mark II, a favorite of celebrities, including Elvis. Wagner infuses his talks with the personal touch, asking questions, and especially engaging children with quizzes and games and encouraging them to contribute their own ideas. He imparts history lessons along the way, such as the location of gas tanks on military vehicles and the differences between WWI Jeeps and those of subsequent conflicts.

While this passion may seem out of character for a banker by trade, Wagner has always loved cars and collected them for decades. In 2008, he teamed up with Mark Hagans, a former client, and together they purchased the 4,100-square-foot, 1930s-era space. "I started giving tours, and it just snowballed," Wagner told visitors. While Hagans and his horde of vintage Packards departed in 2017, the ever-intrepid Wagner took in the military memorabilia of neighbor Jay Borman. "This adds a whole new dimension," adds Wagner. "When veterans stop by, they share their stories. I am always learning something new." As do visitors to this museum.

Address 476 E Kossuth Street, Columbus, OH 43206, +1 (614) 271-0888 | **Getting there** Bus 4 or 8 to Parsons Avenue & Columbus Street | **Hours** Call for schedule | **Tip** Check out another mode of transportation at the all-volunteer Ohio Railway Museum, which also offers train rides (990 Proprietors Road, Worthington, OH 43085, www.ohiorailwaymuseum.org).

107__Wexner Center for the Arts

Complex thought in art and architecture

There is nothing simple about the Wexner Center for the Arts, including the experimental-style building. Originally constructed in 1989 by then-newbie architect Peter Eisenman, its façade emulates the 12.5 degrees of variation between the urban grid of the City of Columbus and the OSU campus location. This off-kilter approach continues with two turret-like structures, a nod to its roots as an armory. An interesting but confusing layout with oddly angled galleries and staircases was exacerbated by leaks, excessive light potentially damaging to artwork and wide variations in inside temperatures. One employee admitted to *The New York Times* that he was initially afraid to walk down the stairs: "I thought I would fall off," he confessed at the time.

So in 2003, Director Sherri Geldin called in an engineering firm. Leaks were repaired, lighting and HVAC were brought up to snuff, and, fortunately for attendees, the all-important video/film theater was upgraded, including comfortable seating.

And the Wex, as it's known, has been going strong ever since, although Geldin recently retired after 25 years. Exhibitions such as art stylings of cult filmmaker John Waters, embrace all media and ranges of artists. They embrace the work of lesser knowns like painter Mickalene Thomas who works with rhinestone, acrylic, and enamel along collaborative shows around themes such as Dadaism. The curated film series covers everything from low budget 'B' melodramas of the 1930s to an esoteric self-portrait of a resident artist. The performing arts showcase contemporary dance, music, theater, and mixtures of same. Lecture and educational programs bring visitors up to speed on current and creative events and developments. Things seem to have aligned for this incubator of all things avant-garde.

Address 1871 N High Street, Columbus, OH 43210, +1 (614) 292-3535, www.wexarts.org | Getting there Bus 1 to N High Street & E 15th Avenue | Hours Vary, depending upon program | Tip With three performance spaces, the Short North Stage also offers a wide variety of shows, from Broadway classics (*West Side Story*) to wacky revivals (*Nunsense A-Men*) (1187 N High Street, Columbus, OH 43201, www.shortnorthstage.org).

108___White Castle Headquarters

Breaching the Albino Bastille

From its humble beginnings in 1921 in Wichita, Kansas, White Castle, a pioneer in the fast-food industry and the home of the two-square-inch 'Slider' hamburger, seems poised to take over the world.

Relocated in 1934 to its current home on Goodale Boulevard, and as part of the Porcelain Steel company that makes kitchen furnishings for this family-owned business, the White Castle World Headquarters, which resembles the exterior of its pristine vanilla-and-chrome restaurants, is usually off-limits to the public. However, the lobby is filled with decades of memorabilia and photos, including a hamburger presented to founder Billy Ingram in 1957.

That's about to change. White Castle is building a brand-new headquarters building on its grounds with Google-like amenities – a lobby with a spiral staircase, spaces where workers can play games and relax, and even a 'throne room' where visitors can enjoy the menu along with rotating displays. 250 apartments, a 70,000-square-foot office building, a community center/event space, and an amphitheater are also in the works. Who says fast food can't be a lifestyle choice?

Dedicated employees and customers are treated royally there. Along with health insurance, paid vacations, and other perks, White Castle has one of the highest worker retention rates in an industry known for turnover – many of the executives started out flipping burgers. Menu aficionados, known as Cravers, have their own honorary club, the Cravers Hall of Fame. Only about 240 or so White Castle fans have been selected since its establishment in 2001 from thousands of "personal, funny and heartfelt stories" submitted each year, says the company's website. Honorees receive an all-expense paid trip either to the Mother Ship in Columbus or an annual meeting, where they are inducted, wined, and dined. On sliders, of course.

Address Original headquarters, 555 West Goodale Boulevard, Columbus, OH 43215; new headquarters, 2106 N High Street Columbus, OH 43201, www.whitecastle.com | **Getting there** To original: Bus 3 to 582 W Goodale S, head east; to new: bus 102 to N High Street & W Woodruff Avenue | **Hours** By appointment | **Tip** For a deep dive into company history, as well as a decade-spanning collection of restaurant plates, mugs, glassware, uniforms and more, visit the White Castle display at the Ohio History Center (800 E 17th Avenue, Columbus, OH 43211, www.ohiohistory.org).

109__Wonder Bread Factory
Sleeping with the loaves

When the Italian Village-based Wonder Bread Factory closed its doors in 2009 after almost 100 years of operation, displaced workers and locals alike expressed concern over the fate of the historic structure. "It's a fairly unique building," Larry Totzke, president of the Italian Village Society told *The Columbus Dispatch*. "You can't just turn it into condos." But that's exactly what happened – almost.

The 70,000-square-foot factory was divided into some 66 apartments with 48 different open-loft layouts, and most rents ranging skyward of $1500 a month. And along with keeping elements of the original structure – brick and concrete block walls, exposed rafters and ductwork, huge windows, dough troughs used for planters – developer Kevin Lykens added the latest in appliances and other modern touches. The massive neon Wonder Bread sign, an iconic Columbus landmark, was lit again, this time as a beacon for residents and visitors.

People also feared missing the delicious bread smell that wafted across the I-670 and 71 freeways and nearby neighborhoods. But the aroma of fresh-baked goods continued to permeate the air for another decade until the real source, a bakery from a nearby Kroger, also closed.

Constructed in 1916, the building began life as the Columbus Bread Company and was acquired by Wonder a few years later. It had been expanded several times, at one point employing hundreds of workers, which created quite an architectural challenge during the apartment redesign. By 2000, however, the factory was down to about 70 employees and churned out only hamburger and hot dog buns. Today Wonder Bread is now part of Flowers Foods, located in Thomasville, GA, which also produces Nature's Own organic breads and Tastykakes.

Still, Wonder's presence here is missed, if only for the now-shuttered factory outlet stores that used to sell four loaves for a dollar.

Address 727 N 4th Street, Columbus, OH 43215 | Getting there Bus 4 to N 4th Street & Lincoln Street | Hours From the outside only | Tip Located in the same building, the friendly sports bar City Tavern serves up a grilled PB&J à la mode as homage to its Wonder Bread roots (697 N 4th Street, Columbus, OH 43215, www.citytaverncolumbus.com).

110_Woody Hayes Athletic Center

Exercising the right to win

A stern looking statue of Woody Hayes greets all comers to his namesake athletic center. After a brilliant, if controversial, coaching career, the irascible but loyal Hayes punched a member of the opposing team during the 1978 Gator Bowl, when the player ran out of bounds into the Ohio State sideline. Hayes was fired, and OSU lost the game.

But while Hayes might have benefited from anger management, the Woody Hayes Athletic Center (WHAC) might not be standing today. Built on three National Championships and 13 Big Ten titles during Hayes's 28-season coaching career, the sports venue provided the groundwork for a football machine that went on to garner dozens of Big Ten and National Championships, Heisman Trophies, and All-Americans and Academic All-Americans. Photos of the latter two, as well as a gee-whiz display of hardware, including a crystal football for the 2002 National Championship and what resembles oversized calla lily for that same honor in 2014, can be found inside an artfully lit glass atrium that is open to the public. But the inner sanctum, which houses the real secrets of OSU football, is not.

But this space is equally impressive. Beyond a long hallway with displays and memorabilia, are some 13,000 square feet filled with state-of-the-art weight training and exercise equipment. Other varsity teams also train there. There's a separate cardio fitness area, an indoor football field, racquetball room, and basketball gym. Hot and cold plunge tubs, a rehabilitation pool, a new kitchen and nutrition space, a players' lounge, and a glitzy locker room comprise an investment to ensure that the players stay happy and healthy. Flatscreen TVs abound, so as not to miss a second of the latest sports developments, all benefits of Hayes' infamous temper.

Address 535 Irving Schottenstein Drive, Columbus, OH 43201, +1 (614) 292-2531, www.ohiostatebuckeyes.com | **Getting there** Bus 1 to Olentangy River Road & Argyll Street | **Hours** Mon–Fri 8:30am–4:30pm | **Tip** Ohio Stadium, more commonly known as the Horseshoe or Shoe, offers tours of the Buckeyes' storied battlefield, including the press box, the top-level Huntington Club, the hub for 'The Best Damn Band in the Land,' and more (411 Woody Hayes Drive, Columbus, OH 43210, www.ohiostadiumtours.com).

111__World's Largest Gavel
Doing justice to art

Sitting in a reflecting pool between the Thomas J. Moyer Ohio Judicial Center and the Ohio State Supreme Court, this 31-foot-long, seven-thousand-pound metal behemoth may pound down any thoughts about a life of crime. Artist Andrew Scott created *Gavel*, and he designed it to represent the decision-making authority of Ohio's governing body. The words *Reason, Honor, Wisdom*, and more related terms written in steel in an opposite reflecting pool further hammer home the message. Created in 2008, the $200,000 sculpture was funded by the Ohio State Bar Foundation.

In fact, the entire Judicial Center is an art lover's dream, with a gallery consisting of over 60 murals, relief sculptures, and mosaics depicting scenes and people from Ohio's history and industry. The work of more Ohioans, such as the Tuskegee Airmen Series by Robert E. Tanner Sr. from the city of Delaware and the folk art of the late Aminah Robinson are also represented.

Built in 1932 to house the quickly expanding state government, the Judicial Center's construction was hampered by a natural gas explosion that killed 11 workers. But when it opened a year later, the art deco interior with monumental lobbies and hearing rooms and the richly textured, painting-filled Ohio Supreme Courtroom were declared to be 'Ohio's Pride.' But it wasn't until the turn of this century that, in conjunction with efforts by Chief Justice Moyer, a team of designers, construction workers, and artisans restored the building to its original glory. It was named in honor of Moyer after his death in 2010.

Gavel is a popular spot to sit and relax or grab lunch *al fresco* when the weather is halfway decent or there's a pause in the ongoing street construction. "It has also become the place to take that iconic Ohio Judicial Center Photo," artist Scott wrote in his blog. "Sometimes you get it right."

Address 65 S Front Street, Columbus, OH 43215 | **Getting there** Bus 2 to S High Street & E State Street | **Hours** Unrestricted | **Tip** Another large public sculpture is the *Garden of Constants* by Arizona artist Barbara Grygutis, which is a group of numbers designed to depict the mathematical and formulaic fixed values used in electrical engineering and computer science (2055 Millikin Road, Columbus, OH 43210).

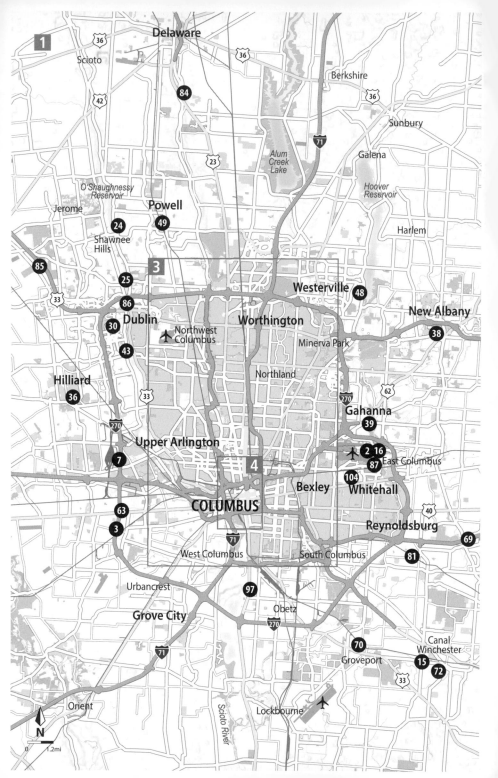

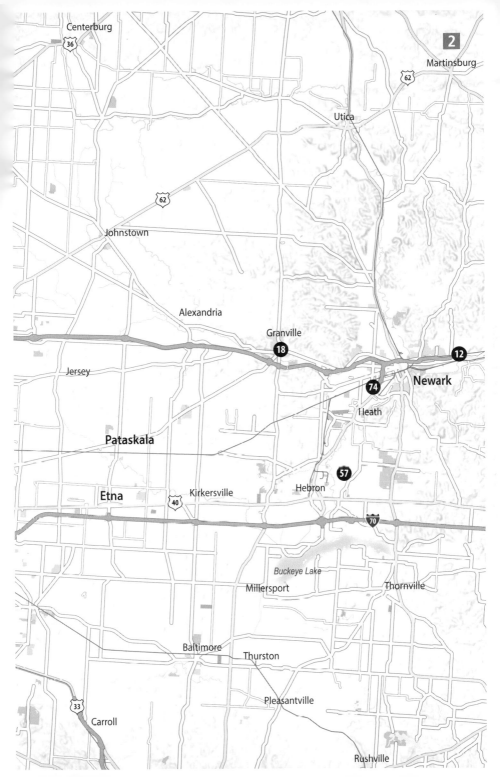

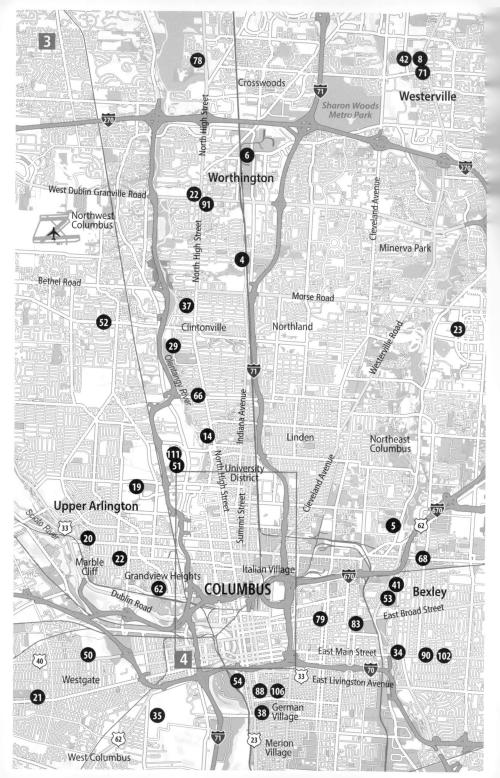

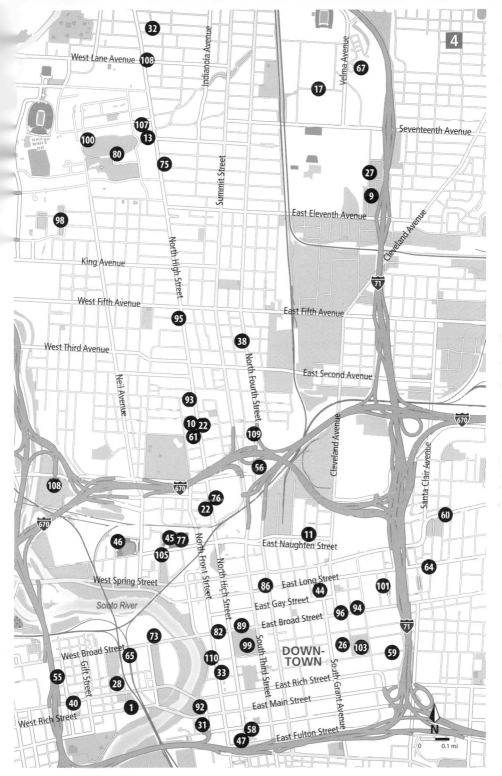

Michelle Madden
**111 Places in Milwaukee
That You Must Not Miss**
ISBN 978-3-7408-0491-6

Amy Bizzarri
**111 Places in Chicago
That You Must Not Miss**
ISBN 978-3-7408-0156-4

Dave Doroghy,
Graeme Menzies
**111 Places in Vancouver
That You Must Not Miss**
ISBN 978-3-7408-0494-7

Kevin C. Fitzpatrick
**111 Places in the Bronx
That You Must Not Miss**
ISBN 978-3-7408-0492-3

Floriana Petersen
**111 Places in Silicon Valley
That You Must Not Miss**
ISBN 978-3-7408-0493-0

Leslie Adatto
**111 Rooftops in New York
That You Must Not Miss**
ISBN 978-3-7408-0495-4

John Major
**111 Places in Brooklyn
That You Must Not Miss**
ISBN 978-3-7408-0380-3

Wendy Lubovich
**111 Museums in New York
That You Must Not Miss**
ISBN 978-3-7408-0379-7

Anita Mai Genua,
Clare Davenport,
Elizabeth Lenell Davies
**111 Places in Toronto
That You Must Not Miss**
ISBN 978-3-7408-0257-8

Andréa Seiger
111 Places in Washington D.C.
That You Must Not Miss
ISBN 978-3-7408-0258-5

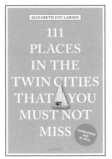

Elisabeth Larsen
111 Places in The Twin Cities
That You Must Not Miss
ISBN 978-3-7408-0029-1

Joe DiStefano
111 Places in Queens
That You Must Not Miss
ISBN 978-3-7408-0020-8

Allison Robicelli
111 Places in Baltimore
That You Must Not Miss
ISBN 978-3-7408-0158-8

Laurel Moglen, Julia Posey
111 Places in Los Angeles
That You Must Not Miss
ISBN 978-3-95451-884-5

Floriana Petersen
111 Places in San Francisco
That You Must Not Miss
ISBN 978-3-95451-609-4

Jo-Anne Elikann
111 Places in New York
That You Must Not Miss
ISBN 978-3-95451-052-8

Michael Murphy, Sally Asher
111 Places in New Orleans
That You Must Not Miss
ISBN 978-3-95451-645-2

Gordon Streisand
111 Places in Miami and the
Keys That You Must Not Miss
ISBN 978-3-95451-644-5

No book is an island, especially not a guidebook. I would like to thank the following people for their suggestions: Linda Deitch (suggester extra ordinare), Missy Cohan, David Cohen, Monique Finneran, Lisa Jenkins, Christine Morrison, Sherry Paprocki, and Rhoda Gaffin Ryan. If I left anybody out, I apologize in advance. Thanks also to my editor Karen Seiger for her advice and guidance, and Mitch Geiser for his excellent photos.

Also my family, friends, and hairdresser(s) with their patience as I went through the process without going completely bald/gray. Also the cats, Mr. Peabody, whose cuteness always provided a welcome distraction, and 18-year-old Savannah, a reminder to keep on truckin'. Last but most certainly not least, my 7-year-old granddaughter Hope for suggesting the dog and cheetah exhibit for the chapter on the Columbus Zoo. S. G.

I would first like to thank my wife Bizzie Geiser and my baby girl K. O. Geiser, who have been supportive and flexible with me during this project. My wife helped so much with the planning and organization, so the biggest thanks goes to her. I also want to thank the local photography community which regularly challenges me to get out to see new things in our city. Thanks to my friends and family who have supported my hobby along the way. I could not have finished the photography for this book if it were not for everyone mentioned above. M. G.

Sandra Gurvis, the author of 17 commercially published books and hundreds of magazine articles, is a native of Ohio and (almost) life-long resident of Columbus. Although many of her titles center around Ohio and Columbus, she is currently working on a memoir/guidebook, *Life During Wartime: Lessons From My Son's Addiction.*

Mitch Geiser is a professional barber and also the founder of @ColumbusVisuals, an Instagram group for any and all local photographers. A Columbus native, he lives in the city with his wife Bizzie and their daughter K. O. He enjoys finding beauty in everyday life and then taking its picture.